RESPONSES

Diaries, and Letters

GW00792188

ANGEL SCOTT

Nelson

Thomas Nelson and Sons Ltd
Nelson House, Mayfield Road
Walton-on-Thames, Surrey
KT12 5PL UK

51 York Place
Edinburgh
EH1 3JD UK

Thomas Nelson (Hong Kong) Ltd
Toppan Building 10/F
22A Westlands Road
Quarry Bay Hong Kong

Thomas Nelson Australia
102 Dodds Street
South Melbourne
Victoria 3205   Australia

Nelson Canada
1120 Birchmount Road
Scarborough Ontario
M1K 5G4 Canada

First published by Thomas Nelson and
Sons Ltd 1990

ISBN 0–17–432227–5
NPN 9 8 7 6 5 4 3 2

Printed in Hong Kong

■ CONTENTS ■

▌RESPONSES▐

Series editors: Angel and Patrick Scott

Community Writing by Don Shiach
Frankie Mae and other stories by Ann Mann and Hilary Rich
Wordlife by Richard Knott
Everyday use and other stories by Elaine Millard and Barbara White
The Wild Bunch and other plays by Don Shiach
Diaries, Journals and Letters by Angel Scott

Editors' note
GCSE reflects some of the most interesting and successful initiatives
in English teaching that have taken place over the last 15 to 20
years. As a consequence it is no longer possible to ignore classroom
talk, or to pretend that 'response' doesn't play an important part in
reading, and 'variety' in writing. No longer can the English curriculum
be sliced up into lessons on 'comprehension' or 'essay writing' or
'spelling'; the constituent parts of the subject are 'clearly inter-related
and interdependent' (National Criteria for GCSE), and one activity
has to grow naturally out of another.

This series builds on these principles. It aims to make available for
pupils some of the best contemporary sources ranging from familiar
literary genres, like poetry or the short story, to less conventional
forms, like community writing. The 'follow-on' work that is included at
the back of each book suggests ways in which teachers might use the
material to provoke discussion, develop ideas for folios of work and
introduce pupils to new ways of reading texts. That is why the series
as a whole is called 'Responses'.

Angel and Patrick Scott

■ INTRODUCTION ■

Diaries, journals and letters are three of the most common forms of writing. All kinds of people have at some time kept a diary or journal. The reasons why people keep diaries and journals are as varied as people themselves. For some people, writing down their thoughts and feelings is a way of helping them to understand their emotions. Some people like to record the passing seasons and remember the personal and public events that took place. Travel diaries are a way of recording and sharing places and experiences. Some diaries and journals are written explicitly for sharing so that others may learn from them. It is not only famous people's diaries that are interesting and worth reading. Often, reading about the feelings of ordinary people and sharing in the day-to-day detail of their lives can be both fascinating and reassuring.

Letter writing can be equally diverse. First and foremost, letters are a direct and effective means of communication, but the purpose of the communication can be varied. As with diaries, some people write letters to specific people as a way of trying to understand themselves. Other people's letters are, like diaries, records of their day-to-day lives to be shared with people they are separated from. Letters can also be very functional and serve specific purposes, like applying for jobs, requesting information or making a complaint.

Diaries, journals and letters can also be used as literary devices for telling a story, or moving the plot along, or creating characters with whom we can identify.

The purpose of the diary and the letter and their intended audience will greatly affect and alter the style and content. As writers, diaries, journals and letters offer us tremendous scope to express ourselves in a variety of ways for a variety of purposes. Reading and writing diaries, letters and journals is an interesting way of reflecting upon our own and other people's lives and of enabling us to acknowledge our common humanity.

Angel Scott

Acknowledgements
The authors and publishers are grateful to the following for permission
to reproduce copyright extract material:
Gerald Duckworth & Co. Ltd for *Beryl Bainbridge's English Journey*
© Beryl Bainbridge; Anthony Sheil Associates Ltd for *A Message
from the Falklands* © Hugh Tinker; Hamish Hamilton Ltd for *The
Magic Apple Tree* © Susan Hill; Penguin Books Ltd for *Catherine:
The Story of a Young Girl Who Died of Anorexia* © Maureen Dunbar
1986; The Women's Press Ltd for *French Letters* © Eileen
Fairweather; Oxford University Press for *The Diary of a Teenage
Health Freak* © Aidan McFarlane and Ann McPherson 1987; Book
Review by Adrian Mole © Sue Townsend 1987, reprinted from *The
Diary of a Teenage Health Freak* by Aidan McFarlane and Ann
McPherson (1987) by permission of Oxford University Press; Bernard
T Harrison (1986) *Sarah's Letters: A Case of Shyness* edited by
Fred Murphy, Bedford Way Papers 26, London: Institute of Education,
University of London; Century Hutchinson Publishing Group Ltd for
Brave Heart: The Diary of a 9 Year Old Who Refused to Die ©
Joanne Gillespie.

The Magic Apple Tree
■ *by Susan Hill* ■

1

The writer Susan Hill, her husband Stanley, and their daughter Jessica
went to live in a cottage in the village of Barley, just outside Oxford.
Her book, *The Magic Apple Tree*, is a journal of a country year in
which she chronicles, against a backdrop of the changing seasons,
the events and the people that make up life in a small rural community.

The extracts that follow are taken from:
**The Magic Apple Tree: A Country Year, Susan Hill (Penguin,
1983)**

Winter

... At five in the morning, I woke to a wonderful silence. I went
to the window and pushed it open carefully. A little heap of snow
fell inwards on to the ledge. A light wind was taking it now, and
moulding and shaping it against the hedges and fences. Everything
was bone-white, under the riding moon. I wanted to go out and
walk in the fields by myself, to watch for owls and foxes and
smell the night smells. Dull common sense and tiredness prevailed.
I returned to bed and have ever afterwards regretted it, for such
times come rarely and the countryside under the first, heavy fall
of snow at four in the morning is a changed and an enchanted
place, the imagination would feed upon the memory of it for ever
after.

Next morning, the snow had turned pink, and the sky was
pink, too, the whole Fen and all the snow-covered fields between
seemed to glow with it, as the sun rose. Then the light changed
as it climbed higher, and on the near horizon we could see more
snow clouds, banked one upon the other, menacing, moving
nearer. I felt excited, babbled of sledges and skis, snowmen and
snowballs. Intending to go up the stone steps as usual to collect
mail and milk and newspaper from the box in the wall, I opened
the front door and stepped out and up to my knees in snow. The
steps were not to be seen, and the stone wall dividing us from the
Buttercup field, below the apple tree, was concealed too, under
the hummocks and billows of wind-blown snow. It was clear that
there would have been no deliveries.

After half an hour or so of hard digging, scraping and shoving
back, we carved a narrow path out to the lane, but no further.
Moon Cottage was cut off from Geranium Cottage, belonging to
our neighbour Mr Elder, and from Fen Cottage opposite, and
School Lane was cut off from the rest of the village, and the
village from the world. Across the snow, we saw other people
with shovels and waved to them, stranded on our island. I wondered about old Miss Reevers, alone in the very last cottage,

2

before the lane peters out into the fields, and how much food we had and how long it would be before Stanley would get to work again.

But I spent my childhood in North Yorkshire, long hard winters were usual; buses could not run and we walked to school through snowdrifts; farms and villages were cut off for weeks on end. None of that would happen in Barley, yet I felt, at least on this first morning, the old, childish excitement.

Extremes of bad weather and being isolated by them does bring out the best in village communities and shows up all the strengths of this way of life. There are about five hundred souls in Barley, and more than half of them are over sixty, quite a few well over eighty. It is a companionable village, and fairly compact but, because of its situation, set on a hill, it is badly placed for vehicles to negotiate the lanes in snow and ice. It was only two and a half days before the ploughs got to us, fast followed by the delivery vans, and before we ourselves could, albeit hazardously, get out, but I have not enjoyed a time so well for years, or felt so at one with my neighbours, so useful and purposeful, touched by that spirit of blitz and blizzard which my generation, and those after it, has lacked much experience of. This may seem a sentimental view. It is not. Of course, we were not suffering any extremes of deprivation, we had electricity and water and food, no one was taken seriously ill, we telephoned each other with offers and requests, we could walk about. In the West country, where many villages were inaccessible for weeks, an emergency local radio station was set up to broadcast news and weather information, and it knitted local communities together, over the air if not in the flesh, it cheered, informed and alerted. We had no need of such a measure, but if we had been in severe difficulty, we could have got by, with a sense of solidarity. The young and strong trudged through the snow to share supplies and take messages, the housebound and elderly made hot drinks and received more visitors in those few days than often during weeks of normal life. Meals-on-wheels became meals-on-foot, the village school remained closed, but for once the pub was entirely full of locals only, and its car park was empty.

And oh, the joy for the children, to live within reach of so many sloping, snow-covered fields. All day they slid and tobogganed, ran and tumbled and pelted one another . . . and at the end of the afternoons the lanes were lined with coloured gnome-figures in woollen hats, the little ones half asleep, pulled on sledges or carried on shoulders, noses red as berries, hands raw as meat, voices hoarse with shouting. It was the most carefree, joyous of interludes, the world was as far off as the moon, and just as unreal, its doings could not touch us. I wanted it never to end.

3

But, waking at dawn on Saturday, I heard the slip and slide and bump of loosening snow, the patter of rain on the windows. The sky was the colour of a gull's back and the snow just a little darker, already smirched and soiled-looking.

The thaw had begun . . .

If you want anything in Barley you go to see Nance and George. Nance and George between them can find anyone who does anything, or sells it or sometimes has a bit of this in exchange for a bit of that. They know everyone in the village and for miles around, they relay advice, information and news. Nance runs her family and the village shop and delivers meals-on-wheels and is the Secretary of the W.I., George is caretaker of the village hall, a spare-time carpenter and handyman, a keeper of ferrets, shooter of pigeons and crows. He knows where and when you can get bales of straw, second-hand chicken wire, sloes, day-old bantams and green walnuts, retriever puppies, marrow plants and well-rotted manure. He has helped us out of trouble with our septic-tank overflow and a jackdaw-blocked chimney, got us a cheap garden shed and wrung the necks of sick hens. George is very tall and very thin, Nance is tiny, brittle-looking as a sparrow. I have never seen either of them sitting down. They have a stream running through the bottom of their garden, and, in spite of the ferrets, they rear orphaned leverets and ducklings and injured tawny owls. There is generally a makeshift cage or wire-run about the place, and a notice on garage or shed door saying 'Do not open'. I like to go and see them, they are good people to be with . . .

The country year is marked by the changes in the weather and the look of the landscape, the Church's year by the cycle of the Church calendar, and the village year has its own pattern, too, following both, and including all the social festivals and community activities, and so the wheel turns, for everything there is a season . . . [I]n all the villages of Britain you find the pattern of the year's feasts and festivals and seasonal celebrations meticulously followed, and the fruits of the earth enjoyed also in their turn.

Every day, from around the middle of October, you may see people going up the lanes of the village pushing wheelbarrows, old prams or bicycles with baskets, laden with all manner of burnable refuse. Guy Fawkes night comes at a useful time for gardeners, everyone is clearing up. The pushers and pullers heave up the steep hill that runs out of the village to the east, Norman Lane, at the top of which is the football field on which the Youth Club and the Cubs and Scouts will construct that wondrous edifice, the Barley Bonfire.

When it is finally piled up and propped around with planks,

like a vast wigwam, a roster of security guards will be drawn up to protect it from the raiding parties sent out by rival villagers, and there is a huge tarpaulin on hand, in case of really prolonged rain.

Because the field is at the top of the hill, and there are wide views all the way round, the Barley Bonfire is also lit to celebrate Royal and National events. But the Guy Fawkes one comes at the best time of all, it has a pagan magic that draws all who can make the climb to the top, to stand in a wide circle around the fire as it roars up and the sparks and smoke fly free. Someone brings hot soup in an urn and dishes it out from the back of an estate wagon, others have baskets of bread rolls and sausages kept hot in foil, and there are toffee apples for the children.

Away from the light of the fire, at the edges of the field, is darkness, and you creep away from it, nearer to the warmth and the people, understanding why primitive man huddled around the sticks he had learned how to burn. As we walk back home through the village, the smell of the bonfire merges with the smoke from everyone's chimney, and when we get indoors and hang up our coats and scarves, the smokiness clings to them, too, and the next morning there is the smell of old ash and charred earth on the wind. There is a smell to every season, and smoke outdoors is the smell of November . . .

Christmas Eve comes. This year it came cold; frost lay hard as iron, the gutters and taps hung with icicles like sugar sticks and all the rooftops and stone walls, the garden fences and the grave-stones, gleamed phosphorescent, like silver snails' trails, where it had rained a little that morning and then suddenly frozen. Our breaths plumed out on the air, our footsteps rang, the stars prickled. There was that curious crackling feel to the atmosphere as it touched face and fingers. Barley lay, empty and beautiful under the frost-rimmed moon. Behind closed doors and curtained windows, in firelight and lamplight, people waited.

The singers arrived, and there was much blowing on hands and stamping and sucking of those red winter cough drops that smell of paraffin and cloves, and then, piling out of cars and off bicycles, the players, mostly older children who belong to a nearby silver band; a trombone and two trumpets, a clarinet, several recorders, a saxophone; the leader played the flute and had a music stand borne ahead of her and set down at each stopping place by two eager pupils. More puffing and blowing and tuning up, a lot of throat clearing. The vicar, wreathed in mufflers, said a prayer, gave a blessing, went home, coughing, and we were off, to the corner of the Old Manor House, and by the almshouses, down as far as old Miss Reevers, whose dog barked, though she herself gave no sign that she had heard us; back up the lanes, marching hard, laughing and chatting, joined on the way by latecomers, and various children. We sang 'O Come all ye Faithful' at the Fox and Feathers, under their ten-foot-high, lighted Christmas tree, and 'See Amid the Winter Snow' beside the iced-over pond. We wished a Merry Christmas and a Happy New Year to ninety-three-year-old Mr Stump, who adjusted his hearing aid up and down, and got his wife, who is ninety-seven, to stand on a chair and open the window wide, and greeted a new baby at Fen Farm with 'Away in a Manger'. Our fingers were stiff with cold and our voices raw as cheese-graters. The church clock struck ten. Some of the children were taken home. It was colder still, too cold for snow. We were glad to get to the Manor House again, and pile into the hall in the old way, for mince-pies and sausage rolls and punch and the blaze of the fire on our frozen faces. The lights went out, except for those of the tree. 'Silent Night', which brings tears to the eyes. A second or two of absolute silence, before the bursting of a log up like a firework and down again in a great golden shower of sparks. Laughter and lights again and a Happy Christmas, a Happy Christmas, and a Happy Christmas floating faint on the freezing air down all the lanes and home . . .

I was working at my desk one Saturday morning in January when I heard the sound of the hunting horn very nearby; it had an extraordinary effect on me, stirring, exciting, so that I jumped up and ran outside, anxious to find out where they were. When I was a child, and a teenager, I rode a lot and hunted occasionally, though I was never very intrepid, and always followed along fairly far to the back, on a fat, sedate old pony, and went round all the gates and high hedges. But I enjoyed it, the whole colourful, lively event, the meet outside an Inn or Manor house, the way the very fresh horses were so giddy and restless, the trays of sandwiches and drinks, the admiring crowd, the spurt of fear and pleasure in your stomach as the huntsmen moved off, and then the chase over fields and getting cold and covered in mud and coming home aching and filthy, to bath and rest. I was not a bloodthirsty child – indeed, rather the contrary, but nevertheless I took the whole business of hunting calmly for granted, and never thought about the ethics of it. Man has always hunted, for food or sport or both, some primitive instinct is still aroused by the chase. We do have to control foxes and I doubt if there are any more humane methods, though actually, hunting is not particularly efficient. I scarcely remember a kill in my youth, and often we did not even find.

When I got outside into the garden of Moon Cottage, I heard the horn again, braying through the clear air, and then I saw them, streaming down the Buttercup field immediately below me, the whole marvellous array of them, men in pink, women in

6

black, and the great strong horses and silly yelping hounds and, at the back, the little Thelwell girls with pigtails bouncing up and down, being steered clear of a particularly nasty ditch. They went over the fences and on up the Rise and for sixpence I could have gone with them, I wanted to have a horse again and fly and fly . . .

When Stanley and Jessica came in I told them about it and, even then, my excitement hadn't died down. 'You should have seen them,' I said, 'it really is a magnificent sight.'

'I'm glad I didn't. All those men and slavering dogs giving one poor creature such terror, hell bent on cornering it and tearing it apart while it's still alive.'

And Jessica said, 'Oh, poor, poor Mr Fox,' and cried and cried, for she has the tenderest of hearts, even though that same fox is the villain of so many of her story books, even though she knows how many hens have been taken in the village this winter, and how he comes round every night, sniffing for ours.

Yes, Yes, I thought, in my heart I know they are probably right, it *is* an unspeakable activity and unworthy of the dignity of man. And yet . . . Finally, I sit on the fence . . .

Spring

. . . Spring is lambing time, the fields are full of them, bleating and leaping, frisking in pairs and trios, playing the way all young things play, and Jessica says how lucky the farmers are to have all those lambs to play with, just as we have our cats and dog, and I say, yes, yes, and then the first, milk-fed legs of lamb are hung in the butcher's stalls in the city market, covered in that creamy white caul that looks so like a baby's lacy vest, and it will be tender and delicious, served with the earliest of the potatoes, the very first, tiny broad beans and carrot thinnings, and I cannot bear it, for the meat tastes of mother's milk and sweet meadow flowers, and turns to ashes in my mouth. I rush off and cook a great mountain of vegetables and an egg or two and that will do for supper. I can still look the sheep on Common Down in the face. But, later in the year, I shall manage the chops all right, thickly smeared with my own mint or redcurrant jelly, just as I feed our own hens in the morning and then go to collect a freshly-killed one later the same day, from Forest Farm, at Hope, to eat that night. I am, as Stanley says, a sentimental, non-practising vegetarian. But, if I were obliged to eat no meat at all for the rest of my life, it would, on the whole, be a relief and no hardship . . .

In the spring, bit by bit, day by day, as the nights lengthen and the weather brightens, and as the gardens are sown and planted, the village comes to obvious life again, and people come out into the open, like animals from their winter retreats. There may be dark days still, especially in early April, and there is more rain and cold and greyness, too, as the winter drags itself slowly away over the hill. But there are some fresh, clear mornings, with the dew on the grass, and balmy breezes on which the smells of grass and freshly-turned soil come, and in May there is real warmth in the sun and all things burgeoning.

Then, all those friendships are renewed between people who may not have seen one another for a good deal of the winter, because they are too elderly or infirm to go walking out, or are not members of the choir or the whist club, the Young Wives' Thursday afternoon group or the Women's Institute.

People walk their dogs without being too brisk about it now, and take a stroll to the pub, and do their gardens, or else simply stand, in the doorway that lets on to the lane, at the gate, by the wall, watching to see who goes by, giving good day, catching up on the news. Mrs Miggs takes her upright chair, with the old, round knitted cushion and her crochet, and sits in the porch, and Mr Harrow, who is very old, very lame, opens his window wide and sits at it hour after hour, and the canary sits beside him in its cage . . .

Summer

. . . If you leave Barley by the ridge, after crossing the field foot-path between hedgerows, towards woodland and meadow, and running along and appearing here and there, before going underground or between the trees, is a broad, shallow stream. I had gone for an afternoon walk with the dog Tinker, and paused, on one of these inclines, to sit down in the sun. It was very hot, very still. I closed my eyes, and the dog lay beside me in the grass. I was reminded of times I spent in a remote part of Dorset, living in a farm cottage, some distance away from any other houses, writing, reading, walking, solitary, as now. But, in spite of the similarity of the countryside, I would never have expected to see here what I often saw then – roe deer. I know they are in the area, there are warning signs on one or two of the roads a few miles away, but it is a fairly busy area, worked by farmers, more thickly populated than those places where deer are most easily and frequently seen, and those that do live in the woodlands around are likely to stay hidden.

One moment, the slope of the field down to the stream and the wood behind were empty, silent, in the heavy afternoon sun. When I looked again, a pair of deer and two fawns had emerged from among the trees and were first drinking from the stream, then grazing. I put my hand on the dog's collar. I doubt if he would have gone after the deer but I did not want any movement or sound, and he might well have barked. Then, after ten minutes or so, the young deer began to play, to chase each other round and round, to skip delightfully, while their parents looked on. They may be pests to the farmers, eating and trampling down the corn crops, and attacking saplings, but deer are the most graceful, pretty creatures and the countryside would be the poorer without them.

What was particularly unusual, though, was for them to be out in the afternoon. Usually, they feed at dawn and dusk, keeping in the shade and ruminating during the daytime. Perhaps the heat made them need water and, once out and in a peaceful spot, the young could not restrain themselves from playing in the sunshine.

After a while, a distant gunshot alarmed them and they vanished into the woodland. We waited, but they did not reappear and the dog and I made for home across the ridge. There was no sound of bird, no sign of any man or beast. I have never seen a deer in these parts again . . .

Autumn

. . . For some weeks, everything looks the same, it might still be summer. The leaves on the apple tree are thick and dark and green, the fields beyond are grassy, though there are no flowers at all. Look farther then. The corn has all been cut, and some of the stubble fired, so that those fields are faded yellow and blackened brown, in strips, and one by one they are ploughed, so that the brown earth is visible again. But the trees are, for the moment, as they have been since early July, dusty and dry, but green, still.

The sun still shines in the middle of the day, too, it is a golden September. At noon, it is very hot indeed, we are still wearing cotton clothes, and the children have gone back to school in summer dresses.

But day by day there are slight changes, subtle alterations in shape, in the mood of the season, it is as though everything is slipping and sliding very gradually downhill, like some great high hayrick sinking softly into itself as it dries. The year has turned and it is autumn, though we do not fully acknowledge it . . .

There is a mist every morning now and until eight o'clock or nine it is quite cold, go outside and stand for a few minutes under the apple tree and you will shiver. There are wasps crawling and droning about all over the fallen fruit at my feet. There is a dew on the grass so thick that it seems to have rained heavily in the night. Across the bramble bush that has grown up from the field on the other side of the low stone wall and begun to scramble over it, cobwebs are strung about, delicate, tingling with tiny tiny drops of moisture, silver as mercury beads . . .

9

There is a smell in the air, the smell of autumn, a yeasty, damp, fruity smell, carrying a hint of smoke and a hint, too, of decay. It fills me with nostalgia, but I do not know for what. It is a smell I love, for this is and has always been my favourite season. They said that as I grew older I should recoil from it, the winding down of another year, the descent towards winter, the end of summer pleasures, that I would begin to shift my affections towards spring, when all is looking forward, all is blossoming and greening and sprouting up. But I do not do so. Spring so often promises what in the end it never pays, spring can cheat and lie and disappoint. You can sit at the window and wait for spring many a weary day.

But I have never been let down by autumn, to me it is always beautiful, always rich, it always gives in heaping measure, and sometimes it can stretch on into November, fading, but so gently, so slowly, like a very old person whose dying is protracted but peacefully, in calmness.

And I love the wild days of autumn, the west winds that rock the apple tree and bring down the leaves and fruit and nuts in showers, and the rain after the days of summer dryness. I love the mists and the first frosts that make the ground crisp and whiten the foliage of the winter vegetables.

Soon, perhaps over one wild night, the last of the leaves on our magic apple tree will be sent swirling away, and on the bare branches there will hang here and there the last few, shrivelling fruits, and finally those, too, will thud to the ground and burst open and rot gradually into the soil, or else be taken by the birds, getting hungrier, now that the cold has come, and on that morning, whenever it comes, the autumn will be over.

. . . Miss Moor is a remarkable lady. She is not very old, perhaps in her mid-sixties, but she is badly crippled with rheumatoid arthritis, and walks with the help of a frame and cannot hear terribly well. Five years ago, her sister, with whom she had lived as contentedly and devotedly as could be imagined, was killed when the dustcart crushed her against the wall outside their cottage. That was Miss Ivy Moor. The survivor is Miss Holly. As a result of the shock, Miss Holly's hair all fell out, and now she wears a not-very-good wig, perhaps resembling the colour she remembers her hair to have been when she was a girl, rather orangey-brown. She is famous for her embroidery, which has been used on vestments for the Cathedral, and processional banners; she used to rescue old donkeys, when she was younger, and her sister was alive, but the supply dried up and, besides, she could not manage them on her own, crippled as she is. So she rescues cats, and feeds the birds, and her garden is a wilderness and a paradise for both in an odd sort of mutual harmony, and there, also, she has old shrub roses and wild honeysuckle clambering up the trunks of the fruit trees, and a muddle of herbaceous and wild flowers everywhere. And the few remaining fruit bushes, from which she manages to pick enough currants for her cordials. Miss Moor drives about in a three-wheeled, invalid motor car, and makes lemonade and wonderful brandied pears and peaches, and pot-pourri and fudge and gingerbeer and lavender bags, all of which, like the syrups, she gives away to children and to bazaars and to neighbours and to the W.I. As a young woman, she used to play the harp, and is said to keep it still in her attic, and to finger it nostalgically on moonlit nights, but that I do not believe . . .

Autumn-time is apple-time and apples make cider. It is the end of October. Time to pay a visit to the Twomeys.

The Twomeys do not live in Barley, strictly speaking their farm is in the next parish, at Linton St. Leonard, but it always seems to me as if it exists in some other world entirely, the Twomeys and their amazing place are creatures from some crazy, surrealistic storybook, from a past that never was and a present that cannot possibly be. I often wonder, moreover, if The Authorities know about the Twomeys.

You drive out of Barley on the Linton road, past Cross Gallows and the Long Barn, for about four miles, drop down an abrupt dip between conifers, climb up steeply again and, just as the car is groaning and straining in second gear and almost at the top, there is a concealed entrance between overgrown, overhanging bushes to the left, into which you swing, over a rusty cattle-grid and then along what is not a driveway, not a road, but a messy cinder track, which broadens out, just as you leave the trees, into a piece of grass-overgrown, open yard-cum-field. In front of you is the small, four-square stone farmhouse, all around are the outbuildings, barns, stables, sties, sheds, and all in the most appalling state of disrepair. Corrugated tin roofs hang askew and have gone rusty or else have grass and weeds growing out of them, slates and tiles have slipped and fallen, roofs are bowing in the middle, doors swing open on broken hinges, or are propped up with old cans and stakes. The house, which might once upon a time have been rather nice, neat and plain and sensible, pleasing to the eye, is a sorry sight of peeling paint work and tatty curtains and the odd boarded-up window pane. You could be forgiven for thinking the place was empty and completely fallen into disuse.

Once, there were animals here, cattle, horses, pigs, fowl. Now, there are none. The Twomeys gave up keeping animals more than ten years ago, though they still go to market, regular as clockwork. No one knows why. No one knows how old they are, either, but they can't be far off seventy, and maybe they are much more.

11

They have that timeless, old-young look peculiar to babies, orientals, very old men and creatures out of science fiction and fantasy.

The Twomeys are brothers, not actually twins, but as near as makes no difference, for they look more or less alike, and what they look like are, roughly, Tweedledum and Tweedledee. What their Christian names are I do not know. I doubt if anyone does, except they themselves. They are universally known as 'Twomeys', and each of them is addressed to his face as Mr Twomey by everyone, and they call each other nothing but 'He'.

Today, I park on the grass and walk around the back of the house. It is very quiet here, apart from the constant raucous crying of the rooks that flock in the belt of dead elms over to the bottom of the far field. I knock on the back door of the farmhouse first. It is slightly ajar. I peer in, but there is only dimness, and a smell. God knows what it is like inside Twomeys'. No one has ever been. It has been owned by them, and their father and grandfather and great-grandfather before them, way back, and, everyone says, never cleaned out in all that time. That's what everyone *says*. But it might be clean as a pin for all they actually know. I doubt it, though. As they keep their out-buildings, and their persons, and as, by all accounts, they used to keep their animals, so they doubtless keep their living quarters. A row of old plant pots full of dead, dried-up geraniums, interlaced with cobwebs and flies, stands on the kitchen window-sill, and outside, a tap has been dripping down on to the stone below for many a year, so that the whole thing is slimed over thickly with green.

I walk over to the big building, a cross between a barn, a garage and a shed. 'Mr Twomey!'

Eventually, one of them, I don't know which, emerges, and just behind him stands the other. They look quite pleased to see me, they grin and nod and bob and look at each other furtively and roll their eyes. This is a characteristic of the Twomeys, they are never still. They remind me of those fat, bald toys with loose eyes and rounded bases that babies have, and which, when pushed, rock over and back, over and back, eyes revolving. The Twomeys rock to and fro on their heels now.

One of them is a fraction taller than the other and he is the one who never starts a sentence. His brother never finishes one, so you talk to the two of them in concert, glancing uneasily between. They have little round heads without much hair left on them and round pot bellies hanging over their trouser tops. They wear collarless grey shirts, corduroy trousers with braces and boots, and they may have worn these same clothes night and day since they first grew into them.

'How are you?' I ask brightly.

'Oh yes, oh yes, oh yes, very . . .'

12

'. . . well, thank you, oh yes, very well, very . . .'

'Is there any cider yet?'

'Oh yes, oh yes, oh yes . . .'

'. . . yes, oh, cider, oh yes, cider's ready, oh yes.'

That is how they talk, interweaving their phrases like singers of a fugue, and as they speak they grin and reveal odd teeth here and there, with gaps between, and as they grin they twitch, and roll their eyes and rock back on their heels and exchange glances.

Everyone agrees that it is best not to inquire or to speculate too closely as to what exactly goes into Twomeys' cider, locally known, as the brothers themselves are known, as just 'Twomeys'. Huge wooden vats stand open in the great shed, and stories go that bats drop in and rats climb up and fall over the edge and decompose and it all adds to the flavour of the scrumpy. I don't know. But it tastes wonderful, mellow and still and smooth, and it packs a kick like an old mule.

The Twomeys have an old pick-up truck which they drive about the countryside from farm to farm, private house to smallholding, buying up apples. They do have a few trees of their own, but nothing like enough to supply the quantity they require. If you have an apple tree or trees and can't, or don't want to, use the fruit, and do want to make 'a few bob', you call up Twomeys, and along they come. They are, I am told, extremely astute business-men. They buy cheaply and make their cider for virtually nothing and sell it at a profit which is compounded, everyone is certain, by being undeclared and tax-free, for the Twomeys do not advertise their produce, not by so much as a hand-chalked board on the side of the road, all their business comes by word of mouth. People drive for miles to get Twomeys'.

You have to bring your own receptacle, barrel or jug or old demi-john, otherwise you must risk taking away the cider in unmarked polythene containers with handles which are lying around the Twomeys' yard, and doubtless once contained tractor oil or disinfectant.

You would think, indeed, that we'd all be poisoned by drinking Twomeys but, so far as I know, no one ever has been.

I take along two gallon jars and pay, and one of them pockets the cash in his baggy corduroys, nodding and rolling the while, and the other disappears into the barn and comes back after a few minutes with my scrumpy. Rumour has it that, as Twomeys have never been seen to go to the bank, and when they visit the post office it is only to collect their pensions, never to pay anything into a savings account, they have socks or old mattresses upstairs in the ramshackle farmhouse, stuffed with money. Rumour has an awful lot of things, about Twomeys.

They seem to be supremely contented men, needing nothing

and no one, neither wife or child, friend or neighbour, only each other. Most of the time I let myself think what everyone else thinks about them, that they are immortal. Certainly they don't fit into the twentieth century, or into any other century, for that matter. They never go away, have no television set, they do not take a newspaper. I wonder what they do do? I also wonder, from time to time, what will happen to the survivor when the first brother dies, for they seem to be inextricably inter-dependent, like Siamese twins, or the face and obverse of some coin. And what will happen to their premises – where cider-making is the only activity and everything is so fallen into decay and disuse? Who will they leave it to? . . .

There could scarcely be a greater contrast than between the Twomeys and the Hon. Claudia Hay, and yet they have a certain separateness and independence in common, she is her own mistress in the same way as they are their own masters, answerable to no parent, spouse, or employer. She, like them, is doing exactly as she pleases in the way she decides, she is similarly different and set apart and speculated about in the villages around, and there is something about her that is unknowable and impenetrable, as there is about the two cider-brewing brothers on their derelict farm.

Claudia lives in the opposite direction, across the fields a mile to the East of Lyke Wood, a good way out of the village, and next door to no one. To her right is the wood, to her left and all around and behind her the Fen, ahead the slopes up to Barley.

I first met her when I was out with the dog and she was coming towards me with a pair of pigeons in one hand, a gun under her arm, and a golden retriever nuzzling her heels. Tinker went up to the dog at once and bounded about and nosed around, while I called him away and whistled and he took absolutely no notice. She, meanwhile, had ordered the retriever quietly to heel and to heel it had gone, and there remained, and for all the notice it took of Tinker he might have been invisible. I am always impressed by a perfectly trained dog and said as much, as I paused, apologising for mine, and simultaneously trying to grab his collar. In fact, he was doing no harm at all, but I was anxious to demonstrate that I had some degree of control – as indeed I do, when the dog decides to concede it to me. 'Look at that,' I said, admiring the retriever, 'that's obedience for you.' 'It is,' she said, and strode on. But, then, she turned and called over her shoulder, 'I know who *you* are.'

And went. I found that disconcerting, as well I might, but when I told the story around the village, everyone smiled and said, 'Oh yes, that's Claudia,' and in the end I met her again, and she stood and talked a bit and revealed that she was a great reader, and so we used to chat, now and then, if we met in the fields on those October days when it was getting cooler and mistier, and the smoke was coiling up from bonfires on the horizon and the shadows were turning mauve. I took her to be a County lady, who had had a good education, for she was formidably well read. Then one afternoon, when Jessica and I went looking for mushrooms and not finding any, she went by, with the dog and the gun, and said, 'Can't stop. Come to tea tomorrow, after milking.'

Come to tea? Where? After *milking*?

So I asked around again and they all smiled and said, 'Yes, that's Claudia! Cross Path Farm.'

So we went. At the end of the long, straight drive is a barred gate, with an elegant sign. 'Cross Path Farm. Accredited Champion Guernsey Herd. C.M.E. Hay.'

We closed the gate carefully behind us and drove on. We could see the farm and the farm buildings ahead, but because the land is completely flat down here, as flat as the Fen itself, and the driveway so straight and because there was that slight mist all around, it seemed to be much nearer than it actually was, and to recede from us as we drove. Odd.

The drive, the farmyard, the gravelled path in front of the house, and the buildings, the barn, the dairy, the milking parlour, all were so immaculate, so utterly clean and shining that they looked as if they had just been washed down. The hedges were trimmed, walls and gates unblemished. I have never seen such a model of neatness and order as Claudia's farm.

When I switched off the car engine, I heard the hiss of a hose, and the sound of machinery humming, and when we went to investigate, we found Claudia in the milking parlour, sluicing it down after the afternoon milking, which was just over. While she finished, we went and looked over a gate at the cows, their empty udders flaccid and soft beneath them, tails swishing against the flies. Beautiful animals. They looked as if they had been washed and groomed, too, their coats gleamed with good health. From this herd, the finest, richest milk goes out each day in large quantities . . . [W]e went towards the house.

It is a long, low farmhouse, with one room leading out of the next all the way along, and wide windowsills. The front faces the sloping fields that rise up towards Barley, the back overlooks the farm buildings and the Fen. The whole place is comfortable, in a deep, soft, chintz-covered armchair and sporting-print sort of way. There are a few valuable antique pieces of furniture – a grandfather clock, with a moon painted on its face, a secretaire, a corner cupboard, and a dresser full of Worcester and Spode.

The two other things I noticed that first day were the cases and

15

cases of books, and the rows and rows of framed certificates, trophies and shields, decorated about with rosettes, won by Claudia's champion cattle at shows up and down the country.

As we drank tea and ate bread and lemon curd and ginger cake in the kitchen, where there was not a thing out of place, not a speck of dust or dirt, I watched the Hon. Claudia, trying to work out what made her tick. She could be anywhere between thirty-five and fifty, though I guessed at forty-three. She is very tall, thin, pretty, in a bony, angular way, with well-cut hair and well-cut clothes. She could be a wealthy farmer's wife, a titled racehorse breeder, even a working Duchess. She lives absolutely alone though she has a couple in an adjacent cottage who look after the house and garden, and a stockman. She has only the dairy herd, no other animals, and a few acres of arable to supply some of her own cattle feed.

Claudia's father was an Earl and a lawyer, a barrister with a London practice and a house in the country. Her mother came from farming families in Scotland, and had a title in her own right. Claudia was their only child and, she told me, a clever one. She read law at Cambridge, though she was more interested in literature, but from her childhood, she had loved the country and wanted to work in it, and when she came down from University, she proceeded to apprentice herself to two farmers, one with sheep, and then a large-scale dairy-farmer in Devon. There she might have remained, on the lowest rung of the ladder, unless, as she put it, she had 'married upwards'. I got the impression she was not keen on the idea, but then came some family money, inherited from her mother's side, 'rather a lot', she looked about for the right farm, and began to build up her herd of Guernseys. From the start, she wanted to have the best and to be the best, to win every prize that was going. After fifteen years or so, she has done it.

She seems to have a large number of friends all over the country, and some family, whom she sees occasionally, but to have no one very close to her, man or woman, and not to need anyone either. She is pleasant, equable, a little clipped in manner, and she talks to children as she does to cows and dogs. In her spare time, she reads. She is as well and as widely read in English literature as many a don, she buys a lot of books, and when she goes to shows and markets with her Guernseys, she spends half her time in the ring and the other half in the local bookshops.

I felt, that first afternoon, exactly the same about Claudia as I still feel. I am a little afraid of her, though I also think that she is rather shy and conceals it behind her abrupt manner. What goes on, if anything, deep down inside her, whether she has any sadness or loneliness, any secret ambitions or emotions, or whether she is simply as she seems to be I cannot decide. There is no clue. I admire her greatly, though I do not envy her, and if I discovered one day that she had a secret life, or a skeleton in her cupboard, I shouldn't be surprised.

Meanwhile, we like to go and watch her do the milking, and to stroke the flanks of her placid, contented cows, and be amazed at the obedience of the dog Trick, and talk books with her. And wonder . . .

It is the first Sunday in October, it is Harvest Festival.

As we walk up the lane to the church, the mist is still thick, and raw, the air chilly. The holly bushes and gravestones loom out from it around the churchyard.

Inside, it is wonderful, it is the day to crown all the year, golden and glorious, rich and ripe, to see and to smell, the old church looks best of all when decorated in this sort of abundant way. Here are pumpkins, like suns shining from the windowledges, and a marrow the size of a barrage balloon, leaning against the font. Here are strings of onions hanging from the pulpit and tomatoes and apples and pears and plums piled up in baskets and spilling over on to the steps. Michaelmas daisies and chrysanthemums are everywhere. Up beside the altar is a table set with jars of preserves, blackberry and damson, apple and raspberry and strawberry, jars of marmalade and buttery lemon curd and dark, dark chutney. Here are dozens of eggs in a mixing bowl, and cobnuts and walnuts and hazelnuts in baskets, and mushrooms picked that morning in the fields where Lavender's horses graze. The children have made friezes and painted pictures and stuck collages, and hung them all down one side of the church, showing the leaves and berries of autumn and the work of the farmers in the fields and of the gardeners in the gardens, and the animals gathering a bale of hay, and a wonderful loaf of bread, all pleated and plaited, standing beside the chalice.

The church is four times as full as it ever is except on Christmas and Easter Days, for people in the city come out to villages at Harvest Festival time, to savour the atmosphere and see the fruits of the earth and sing the familiar thanksgiving hymns.

The farmers we have been seeing in open-necked shirts and old straw hats, on tractors and wagons and combines, are here in best suits with stiff collars and newly-shaven, sunburned faces, and the gardeners are out of their old boots and muddy corduroys and into clean linen.

It is, I suppose, an unrealistic, rather dated service, and I wonder whether it is not smug to give thanks for the harvest when so much of the world is empty-bellied and so much of what *our* world produces is stored in mountains and so-called surpluses, the fruits from orchards and fields are wickedly wasted, left to rot or ploughed back into the ground or dumped in pits and buried. How can we hurl the gifts of God back in his face in that way, how *dare* we squander and waste, or else clutch greedily to ourselves for more money, more money, when little children and old men and women are dying of hunger and poverty?

The words of the hymns ought to burn us through, the feasting turn to ashes in our mouths.

And yet . . . these *are* the fruits of the earth around us, these are the people who have laboured to grow them, and gather them in, and we shall eat well and be warm in our beds, through the coming winter, we have enough to share. There are some services of the church which seem to me to be perfect expressions of certain truths that do not change, and could not be improved upon by being changed themselves, but which *can* bear all the weight of new meaning, in new times, as well as repetition of the old . . .

18

English Journey

■ *by Beryl Bainbridge* ■

Fifty years ago J.B. Priestley travelled across England, from South-
ampton to the Black country, from Tyne and Tees to the flat stretches
of East Anglia, and wrote a 'rambling but truthful account of what one
man saw and heard and thought and felt during a journey through
England in the autumn of 1933'.

Last year, in celebration of Mr Priestley's classic book, *English Journey*, BBC Bristol sent a team of eight, which included me, to follow in
his footsteps, recording on film the route he had taken and making a
documentary series of what we saw and heard in the towns and villages
of England during the summer of 1983.

I was not an objective traveller. There are people who live in the
present and those who live for the future. There are others who live in
the past. It would seem we have little choice. Early on, life dictates our
preferences. All my parents' bright days had ended before I was born.
They faced backwards. In doing so they created within me so strong
a nostalgia for time gone that I have never been able to appreciate
the present or look to the future. The very things that Mr Priestley
deplored and which in part have been swept away, 'the huddle of
undignified little towns, the drift of smoke, the narrow streets that led
from one deariness to another', were the very things I lamented. Show
me another motorway, I thought, another shopping precinct, another
acre of improved environment and I shall pack up and go home.

Some of the time I didn't know where home was. I have never
been more astonished than, in Yorkshire, to see sign-posts pointing to
Durham and Newcastle. I had thought England huge, my knowledge
of distances being based on railway journeys of forty years ago, and
found she stretched no further than a day's drive. I had thought that
North and South had long since merged, and discovered they were
separate countries.

Priestley wrote of a 'workaday world that had no work, of a money-
ridden world that had lost its money'. He said there was a dreadful lag
between man the inventor and producer and man the organiser and
distributor. We hadn't yet caught up with the machines and it was all
a transition. Probably, he wrote, we are going to change our ideas
about work.

I had thought his England would be different from mine, and in a
sense it was, but it was a matter of substitution not alteration.

B.B.

The extracts that follow are taken from:
**English Journey or The Road to Milton Keynes, Beryl Bain-
bridge, (Duckworth/BBC, 1984)**

To Bristol   *August 18th*

Travelled by train from Salisbury to Bristol. I read in the paper
that people are trying to stop the practice of burning the stubble in

the fields. Too often, apparently, it gets out of hand and becomes dangerous, though I don't see why unless a gale starts up or someone happens to be lying in the field at the time. I thought it looked dramatic – outside Bath the smoke cleared and flames like overgrown geraniums blew across the sky . . .

I came out of the splendid old station of Temple Meads in Bristol and found myself on a motorway. The authorities might as well put up a notice announcing that pedestrians, as well as trains, have had their day. I wonder they bother with pavements any more. There was the usual deserted walk-over straddling the road; plainly nobody needed to reach the wretched new office-blocks on the other side. Just another town, I thought, modernised and ruined, and if it had been winter I would have wanted to get straight back on the train.

I was wrong, of course. Driving to the hotel we passed so many fine buildings and lofty churches, such acres of parkland and sweep of downs that I thought Bristol richer and grander than London. And what civic pride the town has – not a stretch of green without a sprinkler, every roundabout a bowl of roses, not a lamp-post without a flower-basket dangling from its glossy white arms.

My hotel was in Clifton, built on a rocky hillside overlooking the gorge. From the bedroom window I could see Brunel's bridge. After supper I went to another hotel further down the road, with a paved garden at the back packed with sunburnt men and women. They seemed prosperous enough, though as most of them wore nothing more substantial than a pair of shorts I couldn't tell whether they were well-dressed. I would have preferred to sit quietly on my own, but I knew that my time in Bristol was brief; if I wanted to know about the town and what went on in it I must talk to people. I tried to strike up a conversation with a woman opposite but she got to her feet and left abruptly. The barman was more approachable. He said Bristol was a nice place and that the bridge was an attraction. People often jumped from it. In the 1890s a young woman with a broken heart threw herself off and lived to be eighty. Her petticoats opened like a parachute and she landed safely in the mud. No, he couldn't tell me anything about unemployment in Bristol, nor had he heard of a cigarette factory. He didn't approve of smoking himself. If he wanted to do himself in there was always the bridge. Seventy years ago the railway had run beside the gorge – it was a pity I couldn't go into the gents' loo to see the old photograph showing the river full of ships and barges and a steam train crawling round the bottom of St Vincent's Rocks.

When it grew dark the bridge twinkled with fairy lights . . .

21

To the Cotswolds

Drove over the bridge after lunch, past the Severn estuary and the grey sprawl of the new docks, towards the M5 and Gloucestershire. There was a plume of sulphur dioxide flapping like a paint rag above the chimneys of the ICI chemical works. It was raining. By teatime we were in Chipping Campden, in a high street with houses the colour of honey and a rainbow behind the church. The hotel had wistaria all over the front and a magnolia tree as high as the roof with three buds about to flower. Best of all, the interior didn't have background music coming out of the floorboards.

It was such a lovely evening I went immediately to the churchyard, seeing that I had been cheated out of graves in Bristol. It was hoped I would talk to a vicar but he was out; so I sat instead on a tombstone under a lime tree. The most important person in Chipping Campden's history, it appeared, was Sir Baptist Hicks, a wealthy merchant who spent a lot of money on the town in the form of buildings, charities and gifts. He built a manor house next door to the church, flanked by two banqueting halls and a sunken garden. The house was set fire to in the Civil War. He also had a home in London, Campden House, but that too burned down.

Inside the church a lady was playing the organ and another arranged flowers on the altar. There was an effigy of Baptist Hicks and of his wife, Elizabeth, in the South Chapel. They were both very generously built with thighs shaped like cellos. On the south wall was a carving of their daughter and her husband, equally stout of limb, clambering out of their tomb at the General Resurrection. This information I read on the back of a ping-pong bat attached to the wall on a string. It also said the pulpit was Jacobean and urged that I shouldn't overlook the egg-and-dart pattern on the border.

When I went outside there was a patch of sunlight on the grass. I sat in it until the shadows of the limes grew longer and blotted it out. The lady on the organ was playing a melancholy fugue. And just at that moment, when I was thinking I was in some cool meadow of Paradise there was a deafening drone in the sky and a Harrier jet, its belly striped like a monstrous wasp, swooped out of the blue and was gone in an angry streak, leaving a trail of black vapour unravelling above the trees. So much for peace and quiet in a country churchyard.

Afterwards I strolled up and down the high street. Tourists were taking photographs of the Woolstaplers' Hall. Two elderly ladies in floral pinnies appeared on their doorsteps and began to polish the already gleaming brasses . . . Even the police station looked as if it was quartered in a museum. Altogether the sort of place in which my father would have had a field day with his handkerchief, blowing his nose and muttering how bootiful it was. It was bootiful. If you could have swept away the parked cars it would have been perfect.

I went into the police station and had a word with the constable. He said the only crime around here arose from travelling burglars. The young behaved themselves, partly because everyone knew each other. Only the elderly and the rich lived actually in the town; the house prices were too high for newly-weds setting up home for the first time. He said there was a housing estate a mile out, but a very nice one . . .

On to Bourton-on-the-Water. We were making a sort of whistle-stop tour of the Cotswolds. Tourists wall to wall; cars and coaches parked bumper to bumper. Blue and white umbrellas beside the river bank and children paddling. More antique shops, more bric-à-brac. More cream cakes and tea cosies and pots of strawberry jam done up with muslin lids and pink bows. The houses were still honey-coloured and ancient, but it was hard to see them for the people and the traffic signs.

Lower Slaughter was almost empty. A slumbering, rural village. No cars, and a girl on a horse standing motionless in the middle of the village pond. A water wheel and a mill, both working, and a baker's shop next to them. The air smelled of grass and horse dung and new baked bread. No sign of inhabitants save for the girl on the horse and a delivery boy on a bike, racing down the little path beside the pond and over the bridge. Perhaps everyone was bed-ridden, or else sick of being spied on. Perhaps they came out at a certain time, corduroy trousers tied picturesquely at the knee, sucking on straws, waiting to be photographed, like those sad Sioux Indians in the reservation villages on the tourist route through the Badlands, squinting inscrutably into the camera, gold wrist watches flashing in the sun.

We splashed through a ford to reach Upper Slaughter. Coming out at the other side, water squirting up through the hand brake, we passed a notice saying the ford was unsuitable for cars. The village had a row of cottages, a church, a manor house, a school, a stream and fields of sheep. What economy, what order! Everyone in their proper place, the squire, the priest, the shepherd, the schoolmaster. Except the arrangement is now obsolete – the church doesn't hold services, the school is closed and people no longer toil in the fields. For the retired and elderly folk who live there, waiting for that final harvest in the sky, it's a twilight home; for the rest of us who came to stare, another museum.

We drove back to Chipping Campden through farming country, the wheat cut, the straw rolled up like carpets. In my day the bales were square . . . I helped with the harvest in Shropshire once, stooking the corn upright ready for the men to bind the sheaves with silver wire. Four bundles to a stook. The corn smelled of old newspapers and filled the nose with dust. The harvester went round and round in ever-decreasing circles, the reverse of the stone dropped in the pool, until all that was left was a quiff of uncut corn sticking up in a bald field. Then the men leapt over the shaved ground, bellowing and whistling for the rabbits to break cover, sticks held against the murderous sky. The rabbits lolloped out, disoriented, stupid. I closed my eyes and still I saw the men thrashing the clumsy, scattering things. The killed rabbits smelled of nothing; they didn't bleed. The men threaded them through the shanks with wire and hung them on the handlebars of their bicycles.

While I was packing – we were off to Birmingham in the morning in one direction or another – I was struck by the thought that I was now a town-dweller and had lost touch with the country of my childhood. I had stared at Upper Slaughter and Lower Slaughter as if all my life I had been hemmed in by bricks and mortar. And yet I remembered the plough horse stomping down Ravenmeols Lane pulling the lavender cart filled with night soil, the hens in backyards, the cows skeetering over the railway crossing towards Tommy Sutton's farm, dropping dirt on the corner by the music teacher's house and my mother running out with a garden spade and a sack to fetch it in for the tomatoes. Formby by the sea, with its Norman church, its school house with the bell in the roof, the manor house in a wood of pines, was once as self-contained and rustic as any village I had seen that day. A nostalgic thought on which I went to bed.

To Birmingham   *August 23rd*

Whoever said that England can't produce enough food for her own consumption? All the way to Birmingham the land was heavy with apple orchards and fields of cabbages and sugar beet, barley and turnips. Every other mile we passed roadside stalls selling tomatoes and plums and radishes, fresh eggs, pure honey, potatoes with the soil still sticking to them. Notices everywhere bidding the traveller to pick his own fruit, pull his own vegetables, urging him to walk into the nursery gardens and pluck carnations and marigolds, dahlias and lilies. There were enough pigs and cattle and bees and chickens and sheep to feed us all till kingdom come. I swear it never stopped, the blooming and the growing and the grazing, until the big transporters began lumbering up the slope from Longbridge and we saw a sign welcoming us to Birmingham. We drove through King's Norton and down the hill lined with linden trees to Bournville. The mist cleared and the sun came out.

24

Bournville is a garden suburb covering a thousand acres some four miles from the centre of Birmingham. George Cadbury bought the land in 1879, moved his cocoa and chocolate factory there, and built a housing estate for his workers, with parks and churches, schools and chapels. In 1900 he handed it over to the Bournville Trust, having laid down rules that the houses must be let at economic rents and that at least one-tenth of the land, in addition to roads and gardens, should be devoted to parks and recreation grounds. Almost at once some of the original houses . . . were knocked down to make room for further factory extensions. Only a handful of today's employees live on the estate. But the open spaces have in the main survived . . . The clock in the Clarion Tower chimes the hour with 'All things bright and beautiful', and ducks waddle across the village green. There's a station with the name Bournville written up on the platform. I had always associated the name with a bar of plain chocolate and was surprised to see it. I thought that if a train came in it would probably be pulled by a steam engine. The ville on the end of Bourn was added because anything French sounded naughty but nice.

Cadbury's factory could be mistaken for a public school. It has vast playing fields of emerald-green and a sports pavilion painted in stripes of chocolate brown and cream . . . Steps lead up to a stone terrace and the long french windows of the canteen. A statue in a fountain stands at the bottom of the steps. When we arrived, the workers, dressed all in white, were sitting on the terrace taking morning coffee.

We entered a Tudor hunting lodge and signed the visitors' book. Once kitted out in overalls and caps . . . we were immediately taken to something called the wet area. It was unbearably hot and there were miles of pipes and funnels flecked with dried chocolate and vibrating fit to bust. The noise was deafening . . . The main activity was centred on a machine with a light revolving on the top, similar to a police car or an ambulance, only yellow instead of blue. The light swept round and round, illuminating the rusty walls and whining. It wasn't rust, of course, but chocolate. The whole operation was a messy, churning, squirting sort of business. We might have been in a cowshed. I noticed that the wet stuff was oozing by overhead as well as down below on the deck, and realised that the din was caused by the chocolate being shaken violently in the cooling section. The machines seemed to run on bicycle chains. Ladies in white gloves, as if at a garden party, sat on high stools looking languidly at the bars shuddering along the conveyor belts. Occasionally they would lean forward and with a gloved thumb and forefinger disdainfully pluck one out and hurl it into a waste bin.

Upstairs to the chocolate-egg floor – fans whirring, eggs plopping, rolling and tumbling down shoots, some naked and dimpled all over like hand-grenades, some clothed in sparkling wrappers with Christmas robins for a pattern. There was a funny wailing sound. Because of automation only five women were at work and their jobs will go any day now. Two women were arranging the eggs on a juddering board, fingers flashing across the surface as though it was card-palming they were practising, and the other three sat on their stools at the far end of the room just watching the eggs being magically sorted behind a glass window. The women sat very still, mesmerised, hands folded demurely in their laps. Everywhere bins of smashed eggs, the cream running out as though they'd been in a road accident.

We had lunch in the canteen – which is still called the girls' room because it used to be the ladies' gymnasium. The bar was a talking point – the Cadburys were strict teetotallers – but then, as the men at our table observed, times were different. They were even making the employees pay for the maintenance of the Sports Club. Land was being sold off, and the Lido had closed down. It wasn't on, they said. The statue below the terrace was given to the management by the workers in 1937 to commemorate the opening of the Lido. The inscription on the base reads: 'One Hundred Times the Swallows to the Eves.' Would they have done that if they had thought the Lido was only lent to them? A man who at the age of fourteen had come from an orphanage to work in the factory said that in the old days Cadburys had treated their workers as though they were members of a family. He had never forgotten being given a clothing cheque for the Co-op to buy his first pair of long trousers. He had never paid the money back. When he was married he was given a house, a bible and a carnation. He paid rent for the house, of course, but only in proportion to his wages. And they got a rise every time there was an increase in the family. If someone died they were given a proper funeral with flowers and a head-stone. Some of the other men looked scornful. They didn't think people wanted to be treated like poor relations, not when they were helping to make profits. The state provided that sort of patronage now, even though everyone chipped in to pay for it. They still got a bible and a carnation. All the same, they agreed the atmosphere wasn't what it was. People came from all over to work and rushed off again as soon as the hooter went. That was why the Sports Club was in financial difficulties. And there were kids from University telling the older men what to do and getting it wrong. They didn't mind too much about automation, though it was hard on the younger generation. They themselves would be able to retire at fifty-five with a lump sum and a good pension. Time to do something with the garden.

In Cobb Lane, still in Bournville, stands the Serbian church of St Lazar, built in the traditional fourteenth-century Byzantine style, and a worshipping place for Yugoslavian exiles. It is run, if that is the word, by Father Milenko Zebic, a dramatically handsome man with a black beard. The church was built by its own congregation and stands among trees with Father Zebic's bungalow tucked away at the back. We sat on a bench outside and talked. He wore a black pie-man's hat and a black gown. Watching us at a respectful distance was another man, caretaker both of the church and Father Zebic; he had once been a judge. Father Zebic explained to me that the Serbian Orthodox church was one of fifteen self-governing churches sacramentally and doctrinally united as the Holy Eastern Orthodox Catholic and Apostolic Church. The title derives from an unbroken apostolic tradition which was preserved in its purest form after the great schism in 1054 by the Christians living in the East Roman Empire. Little the wiser, I asked him if it was anything like Protestantism and he said no, nothing like it . . . When I mentioned that I had just visited Cadburys he said that in a sense the firm was the reason for his being here. During the First World War Dame Elizabeth Cadbury had cared for and educated thirty Serbian children in Bournville, refugees from the Austrian-Hungarian occupation. He went on to talk about the factory and about man's place in the world, and he was so forceful, so inspired and glowing, that I couldn't even object when he argued that work, any old work, gave a man dignity. Even sweeping the floor was an act of dignity. I asked him what he thought of the bomb; he brushed it aside as another irrelevance. He took me into his beautiful church, painted in blue and scarlet and gold, and he and the Judge and another man sang a part of the service, wailing and chanting and fixing luminous eyes on the luminous cross above the altar. There were no pews. Later he explained that sitting down was a purely modern distortion of worship. Who would ever sit down in the presence of God. I left feeling uplifted and somewhat emotional. Of course that's the trick of religion. Everyone wants to be good and love God and be saved in return.

August 25th

To Longbridge, home of the Maestro and the Metro motor-cars. I was given a lecture first. The firm made coffins in the First World War and machine guns in the Second . . . The company's first car was built in six months by twenty people. They now make six-and-a-half thousand Metro bodies a week. It used to take eighty men to weld one section and now it takes thirteen. This is because of automation and the robots.

I watched the robots making holes in door panels. They have long rubbery necks made of cable wire, red and blue like veins, and a spiky little black head on top with a beak for a mouth. The cars move in on conveyors; the robots dip their delicate heads and bite the panels in a fizzle of sparks. Then the car moves on and the robot folds its head under its yellow box of a wing and waits for the next one.

Further along other robots welded car bodies – seventy-two spot-welds a minute, or God knows, perhaps it was a second. Nothing here of bird or insect, flamingo or preying mantis, just a gang bang of steel rods, thrusting and grinding amid dull explosions and crackles of lightening. All the cars seemed to be screaming, as well they might.

There were very few men on the shop floor, and they were riding butchers' bikes, delivering cans of oil and rolls of adhesive tape. I spoke to one who said that Birmingham's unemployment figures were higher than the national average. It was running at eighteen per cent. He felt sorry for his lad who had left school and hadn't a chance of a job. Couldn't he use his influence, I said, and get him work here. What influence? he asked. His lad never got up until the late afternoon, as though he was an invalid, or on nights. Nothing to do but stay in bed all day and watch videos into the small hours. He didn't know why things were in such a state unless it was because we had always been best at everything and hadn't bothered to keep pace technologically. We'd left it a bit late, he thought. Even the robots weren't going to save us.

I was thinking about the man's son when we drove to Castlevale Estate. Fifty years ago Priestley referred to the young unemployed as 'playboys with nothing to play at.' But at least they had a structure of home and chapel to support them, however rigid and wanting. Nothing then could surely match the degradation of being out of work and an inhabitant of Castlevale.

The estate is made up of forty or so fifteen-storey blocks dumped in a field outside Birmingham. The police patrol in pairs; the alsatian dogs run in packs. Very few cars here, certainly no Maestros or Metros. And not much of a bus service by all accounts. What a farcical piece of planning. Fifty years ago people migrated to the suburbs because there was a cheap and efficient railway service to transport them to and from work. Not that a railway station in Castlevale would be of much use in that respect. Eighteen thousand people, mostly unemployed, living on a square mile of land. The long road that now zigzags between the high-rise buildings was once a runway for an aeroplane factory. The planes used to trundle off the construction lines and roll straight to the horizon. Not a cinema or a library to be seen, let alone proper shops, and only one small pub, 'The Artful Dodger', with its windows boarded up because they've been smashed so many times.

We saw yet another shopping precinct, all but derelict, with outdoor stalls set up by Asian traders from the Sparksbrook area selling cheap shirts and cut-price underpants, and shoes that had fallen off lorries. A man was selling frozen food from the back of a van hung with a tattered curtain. 'Not one apple pancake, slightly broken, not two, but six for forty pence, take it or leave it. Chicken pieces, mixed veg, pizzas – five for a quid, give the kids a treat!' Everyone bought his goods. He came every week, so they must have been eatable. His partner Syd was behind the curtain. We never saw Syd, only his hand thrusting out steak-and-kidney pies and packets of short-crust pastry solid as bricks.

We asked permission to go up onto one of the roofs to film an aerial view. When we stopped on the ninth floor an old man ran into the lift brandishing a stick, threatening to break the neck of the bastard who had rung his bell for the umpteenth time that day . . .

From the roof I could see an industrial sprawl of factories and gasometers and chimneys – British Telecom, Jaguar Cars, Dunlop's Chemical Division.

I wouldn't fancy living in one of those top-floor flats. Not without wings. I remembered the orphan man at Cadbury's chocolate factory who had spoken so wistfully of the past and of his first pair of long trousers, and his work-mates who had been scornful of such hand-outs. If I had to choose between private patronage and State Welfare, Bournville versus Castlevale, I know which it would be, even if it meant dropping a curtsey and signing the pledge.

An ice-cream van came crawling up the runway, playing a tune; the children streamed like ants towards it . . .

In the afternoon I went to Ladypool Road, Sparksbrook, a run-down neighbourhood mostly inhabited by Asians and West Indians. The High Street had survived but the houses in the side roads had been knocked down or else boarded up with sheets of corrugated iron. Brick fields dumped with old sofas and arm-chairs, and a man with a face as fierce as a hill tribesman, profile like an eagle, sitting out in the weeds and the sun. The High Street was filled with a procession of men in turbans, women in saris and baggy muslin trousers, children dressed as fairies. Trinkets and rings and bangles in the windows of the shops, yams and roots of ginger and pomegranates laid out on the pavements. There was a poster advertising the shopping of luggage across the world. For fifty pounds I could have sent a trunk of possessions to Kingstown, Jamaica. Every other shop sold material shot with threads of silver and gold. On the doorstep of the old Co-op a little girl sat decked out like a princess, rings on her fingers, bells on her toes, and jewel in her nostril.

Much better than Castlevale, while the sun lasts . . .

To Newcastle-upon-Tyne   *October 2nd*

This morning we drove down to the quayside under the green struts of the High Level Bridge. All the people who had been at the shopping precinct had now come down to the river to spend. Such big babies being pushed in prams, all eating chips from little cardboard trays. The traders were selling much the same sort of essential goods as anywhere else, nylon tiger-skin rugs, fur snakes as draught stoppers; there was a pet stall littered with puppies rolling in sawdust and diarrhoea, and birds in cages, and rats. 'Take one home,' urged the stall-holder. 'Give the mother-in-law a treat!'

. . . Going to my [hotel] I keep passing bearded gentlemen who roll rather than walk. I've been told they're Norwegian sea-captains.

From my window I have a view of the cemetery of St John the Baptist Church, and only a small slice of motorway. Went to sleep last night to the sound of bag-pipes.

October 3rd

Up the Tyne in a police launch, the wind gone and the sun warm. The river was empty and shone like silver paper. We set off from the High Level Bridge and went up water as far as the Swan Hunter shipyards.

The past was laid out on the banks of the Tyne like exhibits in a museum – Palmers, Vickers Armstrong, the Baltic Flour Mills, Dunston's Yard and the Coal Staithes. All in ruins with weeds growing, or about to be demolished, or else rotting in the water. And a whole community, Scotswood Road that led to Blaydon Races, erased from the landscape and replaced with little concrete blocks, the shops wiped away, the pubs, the race-track, all those boundaries and symbols and monuments pulverised into dust. Nothing left of the yards or the mills or the factories but heaps of bricks and broken timbers, flights of steps going nowhere among clumps of pussy-willow, and six arched windows in the wall of a warehouse trembling and standing firm under the brutal clout of a black cannonball swinging through the air on the end of a chain. There used to be glass-works, saltpetre factories, engineering shops, tar-makers, gun-powder wharves, houses, churches; nothing left but rubble. In the naval shipyards where they built the battleship *George V* the slipways have sprouted bushes. Cormorants, wings hunched like vultures, perch on a dung-heap bulge of rusted chains.

We passed a floating platform with a primrose-coloured crane on it, and behind that an aircraft-carrier built for the Shah and never delivered because the Ayatollah took over. The floating crane belongs to the Swedes or to the Norwegians; Swan Hunters hires it when there's something heavy to be lifted.

The police patrol the river to take care of small craft and oil slicks, and to fish out the suicides. There have been thirty-six of those in two years. It doesn't seem all that many, actually. We came alongside a tumbled-down soap factory, swung in a circle past a bobbing armchair and made for the bridge again. Because there aren't any ships the salmon have come back to the Tyne.

I had lunch in a pub with the singer Alan Hall. The publican, Bill, had once managed The Hydraulic Crane, a house on the Scotswood Road. He said there had been sixty pubs in that one road. The bosses, he said, had taken everything away from Newcastle, milked her dry, used up the people, the skills, the energy, and then walked off. His first job had been in the shipyards when he was fourteen, catching red-hot rivets on a shovel . . .

To Stockton-on-Tees   *October 16th*

I was standing waiting for the taxi when an elderly man and woman drove up in a car and asked me whether they could help. It would be no trouble to take me anywhere I wanted. I said, how kind, a taxi was coming. When it came I observed to the driver that I thought people were very nice round here. 'We are,' he said modestly. He also told me Stockton was famous for the Darlington Railway and for the first striking matches. Billingham was a new town. He didn't know much about it except for ICI. It was too dark to see anything. I think I went to Darlington on the way to Newcastle, or was that Bradford?

. . . I think I'm going to like Billingham.

October 17th

I spoke too soon. I have been here for one whole day and my impression is that I have landed in hell. I have never seen such a godforsaken place in my life. It beggars description, from the mean little park with its scrubby little trees opposite the hotel, to the grim stacks and chimneys and power domes of the ICI chemical works on the horizon. In between, a mess of concrete flats and dingy housing, vulgar precincts and civic centres, not to mention the winged monstrosity of the Arts Forum Theatre built next to the hotel.

ICI came to Stockton in 1929. Employment reached its peak

31

twelve years ago. The rates paid by ICI to the Borough Council paid for the building of Billingham. It was the creation of a man called Dawson who ended badly. It's still known as Dawson City. His plans for the new town were labelled optimistically the 'miracle of Billingham'. When the boroughs altered their boundary lines Billingham lost its income from ICI. The money was dispersed throughout Cleveland.

The roof of Arts Forum was leaking above the skating rink when we visited it. There's a mean little library with no more than three thousand books, and a car park five times as big beside it.

This morning we went to a café down a side street to see a boy who was going to court later in the day. It was his third or fourth appearance and he thought this time he would be sent down. His name was Bing. He was about nineteen, looked anything between twelve and sixty years old, and was dressed in tight jeans and huge boots, his hair cropped to his skull. He wore steel-rimmed spectacles and he had cold black buttons for eyes, and he was shivering in a red tee-shirt. We had a cup of tea downstairs and then went upstairs to the room he shares with three other boys. They were still asleep, or pretending to be. The welfare pays £5 a week for each of them to board and sleep here. It wasn't a bad room, a bit cold perhaps, but it was clean and so were the sheets. There were plenty of pillows.

Bing, bleakly summing up his past and future, said his mother had [run] off and his Dad had thrown him out when he was fourteen. He'd had a fight with someone and gone for them with a screw driver. This time he might be sent to the Big House. He said this with a mixture of pride and defiance in his voice. 'I like fighting,' he said, but he wanted to be out for Christmas because of birds and booze and parties. 'Parties?' I said. I couldn't imagine who'd let him over the doorstep.

'Don't you want to do something?' I asked. 'Something worth while.' I felt stupid the minute I'd said it. 'Wouldn't you like something to happen?' I amended. 'Something good. A nice home, someone who minds?'

'I'd like wheels,' he said. 'That's what I'd like.'

A huge bulk of a boy reared up under the blankets of the bed next to his. I could only see his arm, stuck straight up in the air, heavily tattooed.

'Good morning,' I said. 'What do you do?'

'Nothing much,' his voice replied. 'I like a bit of bother.'

'Why don't you join the army.' I suggested. 'Then you'd get paid for fighting.'

'I was in the army,' the voice said. 'They threw me out for doing up the sergeant. I got three years.'

By his bed was a newspaper printed by the National Front. It bore a picture of a black boy with a peculiarly villainous face, and a caption which read: 'This is the enemy.'

'Do you know,' I said, 'that Goebbels in the last war made propaganda like that. He'd print a picture of a Jew so that he looked like the most brutal criminal in town.'

'That's it,' said Bing; 'that's what we need', and he paced the room, thumping the palm of his hand with his fist and telling me that it wasn't fair all them nig-nogs coming and using up good white money.

When I went downstairs I spoke to his social worker who said Bing had been brought up rough. He hadn't any control. It didn't matter how hard you hit him when you were trying to pull him off someone, he hung on like a bull-terrier at the kill. You could hit him over the head with a shovel and he wouldn't let go. He didn't feel pain when he was in a temper.

Presently Bing came downstairs with a bundle of clothes in a brown paper bag, in case he wasn't coming back. We said goodbye and I wished him good luck that nearly came out as good riddance; and he crossed the road and from the back he was a little boy in seven-league-boots, pathetically alone and possibly trying not to cry . . .

October 18th

Travelled to the Seaham area to film colliery villages along the coast. Tremendously blustery day, but fine. Drove down a winding mud-churned path to an open space between two headlands. I could see the wheels of four pit shafts down the coast to the left. Behind us a row of trucks hooted going over a viaduct. The ground was gouged out and the mud bubbled up black as oil. The coal from the Durham bed comes up into the sea and the waves tumble it onto the shore. The water is black too and there's a smell of coal on the wind. It's not the sort of place to take the children for a paddle. There were two or three men further along the beach picking up coal in their hands. They had buckets on the handlebars of their bikes and they stooped against the wind and the flying spray as if they hunted for pearls . . .

Seaham was a small place, almost in the sea. It had modern buildings and its inhabitants were bent like trees against the wind. The coal trucks used to come right up into the main street.

I went to the new library next door to the Chip Buttie Snax Bar and asked where the museum was. There wasn't one, but at the far end of the tiny library with its books of outsize print for readers with difficulties, and its magazines and leaflets on how to get benefits, there was a model of the town as it was a hundred years ago, laid out on a trestle table. It was a perfect little place, with a Baptist chapel, the Adam and Eve gardens, its Working Men's Institute, Swine Bank Cottages, and a Town Hall and a harbour. 'Anything left outside?' I asked. 'No,' they said.

So I looked up some old newspapers and I found a fragment of a life-story told by a man to a local reporter:

We had very hard times, we did. People now complain about the price of a funeral. They can afford maybe one car, and the hearse. I can remember when people couldn't afford the hearse. I've seen the coffin brought out into the street and laid across two chairs. Then there'd be a bit of a service and the neighbours would rally round and carry the coffin to the cemetery. There was some wonderful people in our street and queer ones as well. The Police had to go down two at a time. I've seen on a summer's evening a man called Giler with his melodeon and one called Thompson with a violin, along with the women out dancing. I've seen married women skipping away. I've seen women fighting too! Mind they used to fight like men. No pulling hair out; they used to square up like the men.

When I was a boy I worked at Thompson's Red Stamp store, at the Meadow Dairy and later at the Maypole stores. I started at eight o'clock and sometimes went on until ten o'clock at night, for the bold sum of nine and six a week. Then I went down the pit. I enjoyed being down the pit though the conditions were terrible. During the First World War when volunteers were needed at Sunderland shipyards, the miners went to the shipyards but the tradesmen there wouldn't teach them anything, wouldn't let them into the secrets. The reverse happened when the shipyards had a bad time! The men came to the pits and the pit-men showed them how to go on.

Affluence has ruined many things that used to be; like the grounding of basic principles of decency and honour and welfare. I think the State does too much for people. Perhaps it's the position of the houses. They used to be built closer to each other. Now they're separate, or up in the air. I would say the position of the old houses made for a better relationship with people.

When I came out . . . I tried to talk to some old people at first hand but there didn't seem to be any about. Just youngsters chucking stones, and an old woman carrying a coal bucket.

Driving back, Stockton was a child's drawing on the skyline, black spider chimneys and gantries and cooling shafts. Smoke pouring out like dirty milk and a shaft of light hitting the smoke and turning it icy blue.

To ICI into a guarded compound with security patrols and check-points. We had to leave our matches and lighters at the main gates. Drove down a corridor of white cylinders labelled 'Highly Inflammable', past snakes of pipes and moats of water, the steam hissing and stinking as though from a cauldron of boiling bones, past the stacks of the Propane import system and the Naptha storage tanks to an oil gantry at a dock. A mysterious lady in high heels carried a suitcase down between the pipes, vanished in steam, and appeared again on a gangplank, struggling upwards against the wind.

The river was lined with stacks and cranes and conveyor shoots. In a funny way the view was impressive, awful and grand; industrial power on a monumental scale.

On the way back to the main gates we came to a messy field ringed by pylons and railway lines. Two hundred cows cropped what was left of the dirty grass littered with rags and plastic bags and rusty pipes. On a dirty pond, beside which the lorries thundered, swans floated up and down. Rubbish dumps with crows pecking, steam squeezing into the air and turning the cows into highland cattle. The light fell like a waterfall from a heap of grey clouds.

In the evening we went to Norton Hall, a pleasant old building which is now a club for the management staff of ICI. It's in a village-square of well-kept houses, with a green and a duck-pond. It bears no resemblance to the rest of Billingham and is hidden by lofty trees . . .

October 24th

I sat in my motel room with the teasmade blowing steam and tried to come to some conclusion now that my journey was over and I was going home. I thought of large issues: eight wars in the world this year alone and enough nuclear warheads to drop the equivalent of five hundred pounds of explosives on every man, woman and child on earth. I thought of small issues: the integration of schools, a bath and hot running water for the residents of Liverpool 8. I thought of the clam-fishers, the forge-workers and the fire-eaters, the Bishop and his 'flickers of hope', the brides of Manchester, the Asians of Bradford, the Polish girl in the graveyard and Father Zebic in Bournville. I thought of that vicious little boy in Stockton-on-Tees and those inhabitants of Whitley Bay who had sung 'Land of Hope and Glory'. And I came to the conclusion, such as it is, that the English are a surprising people. How tolerant they are, how extremely eccentric, and how variously they live in the insular villages, the cosy cathedral towns, the brutal wastes of the northern cities. And I thought that was about it, one way and another.

Joanne's Diary

■ *by Joanne Gillespie* ■

Joanne Gillespie was born on 5th December 1977. She was a contented baby and a healthy child. When she was nine years old she
started to get headaches. Then she started being sick when she went
anywhere in the car. Her condition worsened and she was finally sent
for tests. It was revealed that she had a brain tumour and a cyst. The
operation to remove them was a success but her parents were warned
that the tumour would recur. Several months later the symptoms
returned – the tumour had come back. Another successful operation
followed, but the speed with which the second tumour had grown
meant that the prognosis was not good. The surgeon could offer little
hope to Joanne's parents and he said that whatever happened he
could not operate again for at least two years. Joanne was given six
months to a year to live. Easter 1988 was the time limit – Joanne is
still alive today, June 1989.

The extracts that follow are taken from:
**Brave Heart: The Diary of a Nine-year-old Girl who Refused to
Die, Joanne Gillespie (Century Hutchinson, 1989).**

My name is Joanne Gillespie and I'm nine-and-a-half years old. I
decided to write this book because when I was frightened and not
sure of myself in hospital there was nothing for me to read. There
were books for grown-ups but there were none for children. So,
I decided to write this book for other children who are like me
feeling frightened and ill. And I hope it will help them to feel a
bit more sure of themselves.

It really all started with terrible headaches and sickness. The
headaches started quite suddenly and they were very painful. At
first, I thought my headaches were like everybody else's, but they
just kept getting worse than any headache I had ever had before.
It was awful. I had the sickness most of all when I got up and
did something. Sometimes the headaches were so bad, I just stayed
in bed and cried with the pain. My mam and dad got very worried.
They took me to see our doctor who said it was just migraine
because my mam and nana had it. And the doctor said it could
have passed through the family. We went back home and the
headaches didn't get better, they just got worse and worse.
    My mam and dad got worried once more and took me to the
doctor, yet again. This time when we were in the car my right
side just went numb and I couldn't lift my right hand up to wave
to a friend that I had seen. What was going on? I was frightened
and didn't know what was happening. I couldn't lift my hand up!
What could be the matter with me?
    When we got to the doctor I couldn't walk in – my leg had

done the same thing! What was the matter? What was happening? What was going on? I was very, very frightened and I didn't know what was happening. My dad had to carry me in. My mam and dad said to the doctor, 'This is not migraine.' The doctor replied, 'Well, I don't know what else it could be then.' He sent me down to North Tees Hospital to have some tests.

When I got into hospital, the nurses were really nice. They asked me loads of questions like how old I was, and gave me some medicine to try to stop me being sick that tasted like chalk – yuk – it didn't work though; I was sick all over the bed. I thought I would get into trouble but the nurses were really kind. They put a strap on my hand with my name on . . .

After the scan there was some bad news for my mam and dad; I had a tumour and cyst. It would have to be operated on as soon as possible. The doctor who was going to operate on me was called Mr. Nath. He is very nice. Mam and dad talked to him for ages and then told me what was wrong. They said a tumour was like a bruise that kept growing and a cyst was like a blister with water in it. They said that if I didn't let the doctor operate, my arm and leg would keep going funny and I would have to stop dancing. I know now that without the operation I would have died but mam and dad were too scared to tell me that then and didn't want to scare me.

The doctors couldn't operate on me straightaway. I had to take steriods to stop the swelling in my head. It took about five days. On the day of my operation, Tuesday, May 13th, 1986, I wasn't allowed to eat or drink anything. By the time they took me to the operating theatre, I was starving. Mam and dad and my aunties were all joking about food. It made me a bit cross, but it stopped me from thinking about the operation. I wasn't frightened but I wasn't looking forward to it either.

When the nurses collected me from my room they told me that when I woke up I would be in a special ward where they would look after me. I got to the theatre; the doctors were wearing green coats, macs and rubber gloves. They worried me a bit. I knew they were going to get rid of the tumour and the cyst, which was good, but just seeing them made me scared, sort of like going to the dentist but worse. The nurse was going to give me an injection. She said it wouldn't hurt – fibber! – and that it had a special needle called 'Butterflies', then she gave me the injection. I felt very vague. I saw a man pulling his gloves on and then Mr Nath said, 'Come on Joanne.' I can't remember anything else after that until I woke up.

The operation lasted over four-and-a-half hours. When I woke up I had lots of wires attached to me and a drain and a bandage on my head. I was wrapped in a tin foil blanket and looked like a Christmas turkey ready to go into the oven. I had sticky things on me and breathing machines next to me. My mam and dad said I was shivering and twitching. The first thing I can remember was feeling very, very hungry and I wanted to talk but I couldn't be bothered, so I just looked at things and made signs. My lips were very dry and I wanted a drink too. Later the nurses came to see me and asked me questions: 'What was my name?' 'How old was I?' 'Did I know where I was?' I told them I was in Ward 18. They were impressed. I know now that they were checking my memory and speech. Then they started to tickle my feet and asked me if I could feel it. I thought the nurse was being silly, of course I could feel it, it was my head that had the operation, not my feet. They were trying to make sure I could still feel them, but I was tired and it seemed a stupid thing to do at the time.

I stayed in Intensive Care till I could go back to the Children's Ward. I had my own little room – posh eh? All my family were waiting to see me, aunties, uncles, nana, everybody – I must have been really popular! They were not popular with the nurses and got thrown out because there were too many in the room. Still, it felt very nice to be loved so much.

For the next few days the nurses came in about every hour or so to take my temperature and blood pressure and look into my eyes . . . I had sort of clips in my head and they were taken out on May 16th. The clips are like staples – they're used instead of stitches and helped my head grow back together again. Some of them hurt because they had been put in tightly. When the nurse started to take them out it didn't feel very nice and she said she would only take a few out that day and come back the next day to take out the rest. Because I felt I wanted to get it over and done with I told her to take them out all at once. So she did. Just remember to try and relax and not cry, and it soon passes. I kept a tight hold of my mam's hand and that helped too. I was so brave, I got a Bravery Award – *Five Star* – I'm very proud of it.

The nurses were very nice. We liked telling each other jokes, although I drove them mad with my joke book. They tried really hard to make me happy – they were really good . . .

When my bandage came off, my hair was all sticky and horrible. I had a big bald patch where my head had been shaved for the operation . . .

I came home on May 19th. I must have been the happiest person alive . . .

Everything was all right. We had a big Welcome Home Party in our garden. All our family and friends were invited – we had a barbecue with lots of games like knobbly knees, three-legged races, pass the parcel, and lots more. My mam made a special cake and my dad put icing on it saying 'Welcome Home Joanne'. It was a lovely day.

I didn't go back to school straightaway. I was off for a couple of months but, surprisingly, when I did get back to school, I really enjoyed it – well, for a couple of months anyway! I started going to dancing again at about the same time as I went back to school. I didn't feel tired, or anything like that, but there was just a slight twitch in my right hand which I still get now. What happens really is my fingers curl up and I can't push them back again. I have to use up all my strength to push the fingers out again. It hurts a lot but I don't moan. If things like that happen, you can't moan or it won't get better. You've got to fight it and that's exactly what I'm doing, and it seems to be getting better. I was given some medicine and tablets to take – steroids and epilim to stop me having fits.

My mam and dad didn't tell me what the doctor had said about the dangers of having the operation, that there was a chance that I might die because I was so weak – they didn't want me to be frightened. After I came home, I was feeling really fed up one day. Why me? Why did I have to be poorly? I thought I was the unluckiest person alive. Mam and dad sat me down and told me just how lucky I was. I could have lost my speech or been paralysed. I could have died. Without the operation I would have. It was a big shock. Me in a wheelchair? Not being able to tell jokes or play games or dance? We all cried a bit but I knew I wasn't as unlucky as I thought. . .

Everything was fine for about ten or eleven months. And then disaster struck. I started getting headaches and sickness again. I was a bit frightened but I didn't realise the tumour was coming back until the headaches got really bad again. My mam and dad took me back to the doctor. The doctor looked into my eyes and said it wasn't the tumour coming back and there was nothing to worry about. But my mam and dad knew the symptoms. So, when we got back, they phoned Mr Nath, the surgeon, at the hospital. He said I had to go straight there for another brain scan. My mam and dad thought it was the cyst filling up again. But after the scan Mr Nath took my mam and dad into his office and told them that the tumour had grown back again. It had grown over where the cyst had been last year. He said he would have to operate on me again.

We had a holiday in Menorca booked and my mam said that she would cancel the holiday so that Mr Nath could do the operation straightaway. Mr Nath asked me whether I wanted the operation before or after the holiday – I found out later that he'd asked because he thought that after the operation I wouldn't be able to dance and I'd be in a wheelchair, and might lose my voice. When mam and dad told me what Mr Nath had said, I couldn't really believe it. The only thing I did understand was that I had to have the operation or else I wouldn't be able to dance. Nothing was going to stop me from dancing and that was really all that mattered to me. I wasn't told then that I could die – mam and dad only told me after the operation. Mr Nath told mam that we should all enjoy a good holiday and he would do the operation when we came back.

When we went on holiday I wasn't worried about the operation. I was doing all the things I wanted to do and just had a good time. I didn't know what might happen in the future and didn't realise how much my parents must have been worrying. Now, I wish I could have helped them and told them not to worry but, at the time, I didn't think there was anything to worry about except that I was to have an operation. While we were on holiday I won a dancing medal, because I was the best dancer. I felt very good and happy when I was presented with the medal. I know my mam and dad and sister were proud too.

I had my operation on May 7th, 1987. It lasted for seven hours . . .

I was back in Intensive Care again and once more I had wires attached to me and a heart machine that made a funny noise. This time when the nurse tickled my feet I could not feel anything on my right foot. My right hand was just the same and my mam and dad thought that I was going to be paralysed just like the doctor had said. For a while I was worried but Mr. Nath came in and said it was natural after an operation like mine. I could still talk though and did quite a lot! When I was sent back to the Children's Ward I could still not feel anything in my leg, but I was cheered up a lot when I saw all my Care Bears with bandages and oxygen masks on. My dad called them the 'Intensive Care Bears' . . .

While I was feeling strange I had to use the bedpan which was horrible – I hated it. Every time I went on it I wet the bed. I was determined to go to the proper toilet. I couldn't walk properly, so I had to just put up with it for a little while, but as soon as my leg began to get a little stronger I was determined to use the toilet. I leaned on my mam and made myself walk to the toilet and every day I got stronger – I didn't get in a wheelchair because I fought it. My mam was determined to help me as well, and she didn't mind – and I was glad. The nurses didn't want me to as they said I wasn't even allowed out of bed and I had a bit of an argument with them because I insisted and refused to use a bedpan. Day after day my right arm and leg recovered more feeling. Soon I could walk to the toilet just holding my mam's hand. It was a great feeling!

Again I had to have clips or staples in my head and I had them taken out on May 12th. Some of them came out easily and I got another Bravery Award after they'd taken them out. The nurses said I was so brave that I deserved it. The nurses had tried their best to cheer me up saying, 'It'll be over soon, Joanne.' I know they were fibbing but they were trying to make me feel better . . .

While I was in hospital I had to do lots of exercises to help to strengthen my hand and arm. Some of these were boring, so my mam and I decided to practise together to music. One of my favourites was anything by 'Bucks Fizz' — their music is really lively and we made up lots of good moves. It helped to make all the boring excercises more interesting.

I found it really hard to write and I was given a special holder for my pen to try and help me. I also got a special knife and fork with thick handles so I could grip them easily. I've still got them because sometimes it's difficult to hold a normal fork, but I'm getting used to it and am better with it now. I had jig-saws to do, too, all to help my hand to get stronger. I started writing with my left hand when I went back to school because I felt silly that my writing looked so bad. People said, 'Well, you've had an operation; just do the best you can.' But I wanted it to be better. So I started writing with my left hand and found that I could write better with it than I could with my right hand. I think if you really try hard to do something you can if you are really determined.

After the operation the doctor said I would need a course of radiotherapy treatment to try and kill off any cancer cells that might have been left over from the operation. When I started my treatment, I didn't know what it was or how it would work. Just a big word. It kind of scared me.

The worst bit was getting my mask made. I needed the mask to stop me moving my head when I was having the radiotherapy treatment. You have to keep completely still so the machine can take pictures of the cancer in your body and fight the bad cells. If you move it may kill the good white cells too. To make the mask my hair was covered with a sort of swimming cap and then they put yukky grease stuff on my face and covers on my eyes, mouth and ears. I was told not to talk for about ten minutes (which is not very easy for me!) and I had to lie very still, because if I moved my head or face at all we would have to start again. They patted plaster of Paris on my face only leaving two breathing holes for my nose. They put more and more on my face. I couldn't see or talk. It was dark and scarry and I didn't know where I was. Mam held my hand and dad my side but I still felt all alone.

When the plaster of Paris dried it was lifted off my face and I could sit up – I was really glad. I hadn't moved so the first mask was OK. The plaster mask was used to make a copy of my head. When I finished my radiotherapy treatment they gave me it to keep. I keep my hat and sunglasses on it now.

My mask fitted well and I started my treatment on May 19th . . . After having the mask done I was a bit scared but it was easy. You just lie there and lights come out of the machine and they move it about. That's all. I just listened to some of my favourite music tapes while mam and dad could see me on a little television. After a couple of minutes (well, it seemed like that to me anyway), it was finished and I didn't know what I'd been worrying about. Silly me, because cancer cells like people to worry. I know I do worry sometimes, but don't worry too much if you don't want the cancer cells to win.

I had about twenty sessions and every time I came I would help the ladies to make tea and cheer people up who looked so down and miserable. Their faces nearly touched the floor. There were some children who looked really sad and down, but what surprised me was that it was mostly the parents who looked down and said 'Oh dear, what am I going to do, I'm going to be sick.' Some people even went in with sick bowls at the ready. Well, I don't think that's being very positive; I think it's being silly. I couldn't believe it. I believe that if people trust in themselves and God and say 'I'm going to make it; I'm going to do it' they *are* going to do it. I know that some people are saying, 'Oh dear, this is never going to work, why am I taking all these tablets? I'm getting fed up with all this. Why did God choose me?' I believe that God didn't choose anybody. It just happens to people. I feel that if they want to get better, they can get better, but they need to try. Some people don't seem as if they want to fight, but they must, otherwise they must like being poorly. I have only got one life and I am going to live it as long as I am here! *I am going to fight. And I am going to win!* What helped me through this is wanting to be a dancer so much that I have fought and fought my illness, yet I was supposed to be dead at Easter and I am still here. So I believe that if you face it and you believe, you will get better. For instance, I was never sick when I was having radiotherapy. Everybody else was and they were the ones that went around feeling sorry for themselves, wishing that they were dead. I was all right because I believe in *me* and that's the most important thing – to believe in yourself.

My last visit for radiotherapy was on June 17th. I was given steroid tablets because of the operation to stop the swelling and pressure. They made me very fat but fortunately they didn't make me feel sick. In fact, I take so my vitamins now that people call me 'The Professional Pill Popper'.

Radiotherapy also makes your hair fall out – well my hair didn't exactly fall out; it was just that if I pulled, hair just came out in my hand. Sometimes it fell out on my pillow when I was asleep and itched me so badly that it woke me up in the night. So I decided one morning that I would pull it all out and the final score was a little bit in the front and little bit at the back. That was when my dad started calling me Baldilocks. I didn't feel anything about going bald – I just felt it was me with not a lot of hair on top of my head. Some people stare – mostly grown-ups and it isn't nice. I started to wear a badge saying 'It's rude to stare'. Some of my friends still played with me, but others stayed away. I tried to please them by wearing a wig, but that didn't please them either, 'Joanne's got a wig on, Joanne's got a wig on' they'd cry. In the end I just ignored them. If you've got a problem like that, ignore them and they'll just get used to it in the end.

When I went back to school, I felt angry but I found out then who were my real friends and, surprisingly, I had a lot of really good friends who didn't care whether I had hair or not. My sister was helping me all the time and, when people wouldn't play with me at first, she would. Sometimes, I couldn't play with my friends because I couldn't run very fast at the time, so I would play with my friend Nicola. But I'm very glad Sarah was there. Sometimes, when I play with Sarah, it's better than playing with my friends.

I am grateful to Mr Nath – he is brilliant – and to all the doctors and nurses who looked after me. I am going to do everything I can to stop the tumour from coming back. The hospital has helped me a lot, but now it's up to me. My mam and dad told me when I got back from the hospital – before I even started school – everything that was wrong with me and what would have happened to me if I hadn't had the operation, and now I think I understand what cancer is. Mr Nath still hadn't said to me that it was cancer. One day I went to see Mr Nath and said to him 'You can give me a scan, I haven't got the cancer,' but he said, 'Well, you didn't have cancer anyway, you only had a tumour.' After that, I didn't quite know what he was talking about but my mam and dad said, when we got in the car, that he said that because he didn't want me to get frightened. We tell each other jokes each time when I go to see him. Most grown-ups are afraid of cancer themselves and think that children will be even more frightened, so they don't tell them everything. I'm glad that my mam and dad talked to me and explained as much as they could – I'm glad they were honest.

While I was in hospital the second time my mam and dad read

lots of books about alternative medicine so that we could try and help ourselves.

I started to see Matthew Manning, a healer, in May. He taught me how to visualise. You visualise anything. I visualise cancer cells as grey weak soldiers and my good cells as a strong white army with good fighters. I make the two armies fight and see all the grey soldiers smashed up and killed – no prisoners my mam and day say – and I always make sure of that. Then a big waterfall runs right through my body washing away all the dead soldiers. I do this listening to music, sometimes soft music with no words. Then I visualise myself as I want to be – strong, healthy and *dancing*. I want to be a dancer and I am going to be a dancer – cancer won't stop me!

During my radiotherapy I did lots of visualising and I still do it now. I imagined nice things like picnics, holidays and dancing, things that cancer wants to stop, but I'm not letting it. All through my radiotherapy I had no sickness at all and I believe that visualising helps because I'll tell you a story about when I was having my radiotherapy. When you are having radiotherapy, it kills a lot of bad cells but it also kills some of your good white cells. Well, my white cell count was too low, so if my white cells didn't increase, I would have to stop radiotherapy. So I went home and visualised our liquidiser and I imagined I was putting into it all the good food – carrots, fruit, nuts, muesli, currants – things that are good for you. Then I visualised, instead of them coming out as chopped carrots, fruit and things like that, I imagined that they came out as a white good cells. I did this with lots and lots of things and, by the time I'd finished, I had got thousands and thousands of white cells that I had imagined. The next day, when we went to the radiotherapy, the blood count was raised and I was able to go on with the radiotherapy again. I believe now that it must work because my white cell count went straight up and I think that was because of the visualisation. And that's why I always use visualisation. Some people say visualisation doesn't work but I believe that it helps you. If anybody asks me what they could do because their counts are low or something, I would tell them to visualise.

When I was home again I was taking about eight steriod tablets a day and I had to get off them. When I got down to two tablets one day, after school, I was sitting down and, all of a sudden, I started talking funnily. I tried to tell my mam and dad but all that came out was 'blurp, blurp, blurp', or something like that. I was shaking and my voice was funny and I wondered what was happening. My dad took me back to hospital at a belt of a million miles an hour I should say. At the hospital I was given – yes – you've guessed it, *another needle*! I had very bad headaches and was crying with them all the time. I was wondering why it had suddenly happened; I was feeling fine before it started. I was shivering and shaking and I felt really, really frightened. What was happening to me? I couldn't even stop myself. My voice had just gone funny. What's happened? I thought to myself. It got worse and worse and I had a fit. My mam and dad and Sarah were terrified but they told me Sarah was very good. She helped to hold me and wiped my mouth when it dribbled. She drew me a picture of Brave Heart Lion. I still have it . . . My mam put a cold cloth on my head to try to ease the pain.

It had been a stroke and it made my right arm and leg go all weak again. I think I stayed in hospital for one night and they kept checking me to see if I was all right. When I could go home my head felt a lot better. The doctors, nurses and my mam and dad told me that I'd had a fit and I had to do all the exercises over again to get my arm and leg stronger. I got a bit cross about doing them again but I was going to keep doing them until it stopped happening. What I did was, when I got home, I either did them when people were around or I went into my bedroom to do them. I've got another physiotherapist who comes to my house sometimes – her name is Mrs Johnson. Some of the exercises she gives me are absolutely boring, but I can see that I am getting stronger each day. My leg and my arm still go funny sometimes, mostly my arm, but I *will* beat it and I hope I don't visit the hospital in a long long time.

Another of the alternative therapies my mam and dad found out about was the Bristol Cancer Diet and natural healing. The Bristol Cancer Diet is 75 per cent raw food and fresh vegetables. No tea, coffee or dairy products. I think that the Bristol diet helps a lot. I've not been in hospital since I've been on this diet and I think it is the diet which is keeping me out. It does not worry me that children have chocolate bars, sweets and things like that, because I know that they've got colours in and anyway I've never had a filling since I've been out of hospital. I've had an old filling put in again but I haven't had a new one and I think that's because I don't have any sugar, sweets or anything. People think I miss chocolates and ice-cream but I don't. I can have carob which hardly has any sugar in it and soya ice-cream. So I'm not really bothered what other children eat, but sometimes I do have a treat like a Mars bar or a packet of crisps.

There are lots of other things I can change, but we have to look for them. I only drink bottled water and herb teas. You soon get use to them. I eat lots of mung beans and things, and drink carrot juice and whenever possible mam tries to get me only organic food, that means that it hasn't been sprayed with chemicals. That's what the Bristol diet is all about – no chemicals or colours or anything like that. My mam, dad and sister follow the same diet too, but they are not as strict as me.

Because I don't have all the foods that most people have I also have to take lots of vitamins and minerals. My Naturopath doctor, Mr Howarth, helps me with them. I take vitamins A, B, C and E, organic Germanium tablets, evening primrose, zinc and selenium and royal jelly and lots, lots more. Some people think I should rattle when I walk – my mam and dad understand what they are for but I just take them – it's much better than having needles!

Mam and dad also take me to a Support Group where there are other people with cancer. We all help each other and have a good talk. I also go to the Children's Cancer Help Centre in Kent, where we meet other children and draw pictures of what we think our disease looks like. I met a boy with leukaemia and had a long talk with him. Mums and dads get help too.

Laughing helps to keep you well too, that's why I tell lots of jokes. We all laugh in our house – my dad is really mad! We have lots of fun and do everything together – none of us are scared of cancer, we all stick together.

Some people think I don't know that cancer can kill you, but I do. Cancer will never kill me though – if I die it will be because God wants me.

You have got to face the fact that you have got a tumour or cancer, but it's not just you who has it – there are thousands of other people like us who have got it. Please don't give up – *there is a way*, but it is different for everybody. This has been my way, it might not be any good for you, it might not work for me, but every day is special so you must find your way and fight it. You are not a prisoner!

Sometimes I worry about my mam and dad even though they tell me not to. In case I didn't win my fight I told my mam and dad that whatever happens I will always be with them if they close their eyes and look for me. Once I had said that and got it out of the way I could carry on with my fight.

Crying. Crying is all right and you have got to do it sometimes. If you feel as if you have got to cry, please do, but don't do it all the time. There is one thing to remember above all, you have only one life so try to make the most of it. I'd just like to say don't give in, there is a lot to life, there is a lot worth living for in it. I know that because I'm going to be a dancer. Maybe you know what you'd like to be when you grow up. Maybe a nurse or a typer, maybe even a dancer like me. But don't give in though. Trust in yourself and God, and you'll be all right. God is on *your* side, He will help you.

I have lots more to say, but I can't find the right words to say them with, just try to understand what I have been telling you.

Sarah's Letters

■ *by 'Sarah'* ■

Sarah's letters were written to her English teachers over a period of eighteen months during her fifth and sixth years in a comprehensive school. The letters reflect her feelings during that time when she felt depressed and isolated. Through the letters she comes to an understanding of herself and her problems.

The extracts that follow are taken from:
Sarah's Letters: A Case of Shyness, Bedford Way Papers 26, Bernard T. Harrison, ed. by Fred Murphy, (Institute of Education, University of London, 1986).

Autumn Term, Fifth Year: December

When I went to the grammer school my confidence in my academic abilities was destroyed. I would have had a lack of confidence anyway because I am that sort of person but it would not have been as bad as what it was. I had wanted to be a teacher so far back as I can remember and my hope had never faltered until I went to the grammar school. I had believed I had the ability to become a teacher. I loved children and I was reasonably intelligent; or so I thought. My hopes were shattered. That school convinced me I was ignorant, and stupid to have even hoped of becoming a teacher. Exam after exam [brought] low marks and I felt desperate even though I was never bottom in the class. However hard I worked my results would not go up, I had lost confidence in my ability as a person so I had based my hopes on my intelligence. At twelve and a half years old I cried myself to sleep because I was so frightened I would never pass any 'O' levels and so would not become a teacher. From the time I started the school the teachers were forever cramming my brains with how important the 'O' levels were. I became very serious and worried a great deal about my work and 'O' levels . . . If anybody asked me what I wanted to be when I left school I would never say a teacher because I thought they would laugh at me for having such high hopes. Deep down inside me I still wanted to become a teacher but I refrained from letting anyone know. Even though my exam results were not good my nan still believed I would become a teacher. She never gave up believing in me. I think my dad was rather disappointed although he never actually showed any feelings or disappointment. I felt disappointed in myself for them. I gave up. I did not feel capable of the work and that was that. I stayed away from school as often as I could so that I missed most of the lessons and quite often I would spend lessons in the sick room. The school crushed me a great deal because of the cold strictness and the importance of 'O' levels. As soon as one started the school at eleven years old one was informed of the fact you were at the school to get 'O' levels and that was all. There was my sister, nearly two years older than me and not caring a damn about 'O' levels, exam results or anything. I feel my dad wanted her to care more and was pleased I cared but to me it seems wrong. She was happy: really happy. She has always been wonderful at art and English so they were the only things that mattered to her. She was no good at maths but she did not worry. She used to come home from school and tell my mum all that had happened and what the boys in her class had done. I felt left out . . .

Couldn't this school offer me the warmth I needed? I wanted warmth and a feeling of belonging somewhere but I could not belong to this school, I would not let myself. I wanted to belong to warmth and this school did not have enough to offer me. I suppose I did not offer the school any warmth either . . . I just could not believe the girls were happy and contented with the school. Because I hated the school I felt everybody ought to hate it. Somehow I knew I would not stay at the school. Whatever happened I could not stay there. Teachers were at the school to teach lessons and the pupils were there to learn. There was no intimacy. Single-sexed schools are not good schools anyway. A school which consists of just females is terrible because they tend to be jealous and 'catty'. My school was cold and almost frightening. I was frightened because I felt I was wasting my life.

The coldness surrounded me as I opened the door and stepped in. I shivered and felt sick. I walked along the corridor with its cold, polished floor and I felt I was in a tunnel, walking as if drawn by a magnet. This was the aisle to emptiness and nothing. I wanted warmth and security. I wanted to belong and feel glad I belonged, but not to this school. This was not for me. I was not going to let myself belong to this school. I sometimes felt an onlooker, not part of it. I would sit in the classroom and watch everybody working hard, the teacher sitting at the front. I could not believe that this was actually happening. I wanted to wake up and find it had all been a dream.

Day and night I would pretend I lived in another world. The only way I could get to sleep was by thinking until I fell asleep. Even now I can't fall asleep without having thought for a couple of hours. I usually think about when I was a child, or I think about people I know and try to understand them. When I was at the grammar school I was completely evading my life because I felt I could not cope.

When I started the grammar school we had just moved to the house we live in now. As we had moved from our neighbours and friends I suppose I felt even more lonely. I did feel lonely: more

50

than I had ever felt before. We used to live on a council estate, we had lived there almost eleven years. All the children there had grown up together and so we all played together. Our house was only two bedroomed and was semi-detached. It was untidy but warm. Us five children slept in the largest bedroom. It was terrible really, we had just enough room to walk between the beds, but we usually jumped on the beds to get across the room. Often when we were in bed we would hear the girl next door chasing her younger brother up the stairs and then the slam of a door. The boy was one and a half years older than me and his sister was three years older than him. They and their parents are some of the kindest and most good people I have ever known. They have faults, haven't we all? Every one of them was in the habit of exaggerating and being slightly big-headed but they were not cruel and hard. They never meant any harm by it. I supposed I liked them having so much confidence in themselves because I lacked this and they seemed to give me more confidence. They would do anything for us and I think my mum and dad would do anything for them. I do not think you would meet such good friends anywhere else in the world. My mum and dad would agree with that. My dad and sister were not so close to our neighbours as my mum and me. They preferred their own company. If they were happy like that I am glad but one thing my mum and I have in common is the need for this warmth. My mum misses our neighbours but she has made friends with women who are not snobbish like the women in our road. Truthfully I don't think I want anybody to take the place of my old neighbours. I suppose I won't make the effort but I find it hard to go out so I do not meet people. It is not people of my own age who I lack a warmth from. I have got friends like Sandra and Gill. It is older people. People my mum's age. I do not know why I enjoy this sort of company. I just feel at ease and relaxed. Our neighbours here dislike children and are forever telling my brothers to be quiet when they are playing in the garden. During the summer holidays I was sitting in the garden while my brothers were playing. They were making a noise but it was not very loud. The lady next door was watching them with absolute disgust but as soon as my mum came out into the garden she was all smiles. Why do people want to dislike children? Children mess up the house and garden. Our house is the untidiest house in our part of the road, but what does it matter? My old neighbours loved children. When I was young I used to help my aunt Nell (we called her that) do her housework. Out of the children in my family I was the one who lived in their warmth most. In summer I would come home from school and find my mum sitting in the garden talking to my aunt Nell as they drank their tea. I loved sitting with them and listening to them talking. They might be standing on the doorstep talking to a couple of other women from the estate. I suppose people would say this was wasting time but it wasn't, not to me. It was lovely coming home from school seeing my mum and aunt talking and watching my little brothers playing on the grass in front of the house. They were often laughing and joking. As I turned the corner into my road I could see my mum and aunt. I used to run as fast as I could to get home and see my brothers and mum and dad. It was safer than where we live now. Very few cars came there because the road curved into a circle so you ended up where you had started. There were two greens which we played on and we also had a back garden and a front garden. The front gardens were all open but where we live now people have their gardens boxed in. The top part of our garden was a dump but lovely. We had a little house and a slide which my dad had built for us but they were falling to bits because of age and the rough wear they had suffered. My brothers had dug an enormous hole in the middle of the garden but they had hours of fun digging so my dad decided not to stop them. I think this was very kind of him because I know he would like a really beautiful garden and yet he gave his own pleasure up for my little brothers. Not a lot of parents are so unselfish as my mum and dad.

In the evening my brother Stephen, David and Jackie (the boy and girl from next door) my best friend, myself and a few other children used to go to the heath which joined onto the estate and played rounders or some other game. The air would become quite cool towards 8 o'clock but I did not feel cold. I felt alive. Quite often we played in front of our houses and sometimes on the shed roofs which joined the back gardens. If it was hot we sometimes had picnics of our own on the roof or over the heath. We stayed out playing until it was quite dark because we felt safe, we had plenty of playing space and there were no main roads. My mum and dad did not work so hard as they do now and they joined in the fun with us. Sometimes on Sunday afternoons my dad used to take us over to the part of the heath which was on the other side of the main road. My dad used to chase us among the trees and when he caught us he tickled us. All my friends used to come and really he was like a dad to them as well. They all liked him a lot because he joined in the games with us and we felt he wanted to. We ran amongst the trees and ferns, stained our clothes and getting altogether filthy; but who cared. I loved the trees as they wavered in the wind and the ferns turning golden brown: I loved my dad. My dad did so many things for us I could never write them.

I want my youngest brothers to have this love as well. Ian is eight and Matthew is five. They need more freedom I think. My mum and dad give them freedom but they can't go out to play without an adult because of the main roads. They have toys and things like that but I do not feel children really need all the toys they have. Most boys love running about on heaths or cycling. They cannot make a lot of noise because of neighbours. My mum and dad give my brothers their attention, more than a great many parents give their children but I do not feel it is quite right. My mum and dad are older so really it is not surprising that they are not so patient as they used to be and they have to work very hard. Too hard. My dad does not get enough sleep and rest. When we were small and we asked my dad to play with us he would be pleased to but now he seems to feel while he is playing with my brothers he could be getting on with some work. I hate this because I am sure he wants to spend time with my brothers but all the time he feels there is work to do. I do not see a way out of this problem really because rates and bills have got to be paid but I feel my mum, dad and younger brother spend too much time indoors. My mum is always in the house except when she is shopping. We most probably have arguments because we are all in the house together every minute except when we are at school. Holidays are the worst times. I never go out so we all feel everybody else is in the way. I feel terrible when my brothers are fighting. One is shouting to my mum [who] is machining upstairs, they fight so cruelly, they seem to hate each other. They are jealous of each other and torment each other terribly. When they have been arguing all day I feel I wish I were dead. Why can't everybody be happier? I know children fight but surely not so viciously, not with so much hatred. I cannot shut the arguing out of my mind. I cannot go up to my bedroom and ignore it, it means too much to me. It should not mean a lot to me but it does. Almost everything means a lot to me whether happy or miserable. My heart aches because the one thing in the world I want is for us to be a happy family . . .

Spring term, fifth year: March

I am unsociable. Sometimes, when my mind is no longer involved with other people I think about my faults. I seem to have a lot of faults, and it is not just because I am being over-critical. I know I am over-critical with other people and myself but at the moment I am just being honest about the way I see myself. Perhaps what I consider to be my faults, are not faults in somebody else's view but that's the way it is. I suppose some of my faults are not obvious to the people about me and probably the only way they would realise them would be by reading my work. I find it very difficult to accept changes and often, at first, I refuse to accept them. I hate changing from my surroundings and people yet eventually I do desire something else. When the change is created by myself because I feel it is necessary, it's alright but when the change takes place while I am feeling insecure, then I hate it. Although I know it is wrong, change means insecurity to me. I suppose I prefer everything to run dry before I leave it and move on. At the moment I want to change the way I am living. I want to get out of school. I want to move away from my family but if I had had to leave school a year ago I would have felt resentful. I did not want anything to change, now I do. Sometimes I think I dislike change because I am spoilt. Although there are five children in my family, I think we have all been spoilt. Perhaps I just want my own way all the time and change means I can't have this.

I find I am becoming more and more absorbed in myself, leaving very little time for other people. I feel more at peace when I am alone and when I do mix with other people I find I have a confusion inside me. It does not seem real. When I walk through the park with David, John and Nick, I do not feel as though I am me. I feel like I am acting a role and it seems strange, totally unreal. When I walk through the park by myself, like when I come home from work on Saturdays, I talk aloud to myself and I feel completely content. Probably half an hour before I was at work, worrying about something I had said to somebody, or something that had been said to me and all the feelings of tension, depression, etc., become mixed up inside me. Then I am alone in the park and nothing matters any more. People, words, emotions, they are nothing. I ridicule my thoughts and feelings because it seems impossible to take them seriously. That's the way it always is for me when I do not feel weighed down because of living.

. . . I know while I was at the grammar school I used to feel worse, lonely because I stayed at home all the time and remained detached from my friends at school. Now I wonder if I have just got to grow accustomed to living with other people apart from my family, or is it just a characteristic that is in my family? My dad and Ian do not seem to want friends who are always around. I know it is probably very unsociable and sometimes I cannot help feeling guilty because of my attitude towards people. It is not that I do not want friends, it's just that I do not need them around very often. Perhaps I should not say this of all friends because there are one or even two who I would not mind at any time, but perhaps I only feel this because I do not spend much time with them. I find it difficult to understand why it is necessary for some people to go shopping, etc., with friends. I do not like having to tag along with anybody or have them tag along with me, yet all the time I am by myself, I am talking to myself. I suppose that does have some significance. I know that sometimes I talk to myself because I feel self-conscious and do not want to think about how insufficient I am feeling. About seven or eight years ago I used to pretend I had a constant companion. This invented friend was always around when I needed somebody to talk to, somebody to strengthen me, but I seem to have given up this friend for the companionship of another part of myself. There is a continual conversation going on in my head, so I do not need anybody else to keep me company most of the time. I suppose that I am just being lazy because being with other people takes more of an effort than when I am alone. I do not think people find it easy to talk to me unless they know me quite well and I certainly feel awkward talking to most people. There just does not seem to be anything I need to say, yet I often think I ought to have something to say. Sometimes I am with a person and all the time I am trying to think of something to say, then I think 'Damn it! If there is nothing worth saying, don't say anything.' Probably the uneasiness I feel is transferred to the people I am with, which only makes things more awkward, because people are obviously under a strain, even if it is not very great. It irritates me sometimes when people say I do not talk enough and I think to myself, 'What do they want me to say?' Yet with some people I can talk for ages and not feel at all uneasy. Sometimes I want to be able to talk to somebody so much that I force myself to talk to them even though I do feel taut. I suppose I only make an effort when I feel people are important to me and perhaps that is not as often as it should be. When I am with a crowd of people I feel strange, almost as though, I am not me. I feel suppressed by everything but when I am with one person I can feel it is a reality . . .

Summer term, fifth year: April

. . . When some people hurt me I think, 'Who the hell do they think they are?' I suppose I think that with most people, but it is no compensation usually. Sometimes I even wish I could just live with a few people who are gentle and sensitive but I suppose that is just looking for an easy way out of having to be stronger. Why should not I look for an escape? When your head throbs violently and you feel hot, so hot. How do you hide this mad fever? Somehow it has got to be released from within you, onto other people if necessary. I know it is wrong to make other people suffer, just because I have been hurt, but sometimes the pain seems so unjust. Even people I feel no liking for can hurt me intensely. I do not see why I should feel the pain when I know what they think and say should be of no relevance. The other day somebody who I feel nothing for, except contempt perhaps, stung me so deeply I felt almost hatred for him. I do not think he was even intending to hurt me, but what he said, wounded me and I was plunged into anguish. It is funny really. I tried desperately to convince myself it did not matter but I could feel my emotions taking hold of me. I remained where I was, trying to keep back what I was feeling but it was no good. I had to find a retreat where I could be alone. When I returned I felt a revulsion even at the sight of him and I was tortured when I had to speak to him. Usually I do not have such a violent reaction afterwards but I felt so bad, because I knew it should not have mattered what he said. What I cannot understand is, why so many things that should not matter, do matter somewhere unknown in me. One day perhaps, I won't care, and what sort of person will I be like then? Will I be hard and rational? I suppose I need to create a shell around the most sensitive part of me so that only the really important things can penetrate it. I do not want to be insensitive but somehow I have got to protect myself. Protect myself from what? Other people, my own emotions, life? I don't know but something is causing me a pain which I want to be able to force back, before it reaches the innermost part of my being. At the moment it seems so exposed and it should not be like that. I know it should not. I know that the problem is me and not other people, because the pain I feel is not usually intended. I suppose that means I create my own pain . . .

Spring term, sixth year: January

Quite often while I am at school I feel very frustrated because I cannot get away from people. I am alone in myself, in the deepest part of me but sometimes I want to be completely alone. They are everywhere, talking. Talking to me, at me and it just blurs my mind. I get so bored and irritated that it does not do other people nor myself any good. I am getting very hung up about this and if it continues I am going to become even more edgy and intolerant. I suppose it is pointless me writing about bossy teachers because most people are aware of the tension they cause by their pettiness. I just want them to leave me alone. Once I could laugh them off but after a couple of years they seem to have become too much for me. I think my general attitude towards everything at the moment makes me more irritated by this school and its dictators, but they are sitll there, trying to force me into the mechanical routine of the school. Why cannot I sit in the cloak-room instead of the common room at dinner-time? I am not a person who enjoys the atmosphere of the common-room so why am I supposed to rush there and join in? . . .

Probably our school is too large for everybody to be where they want to be. I do not know. One morning I had been in this school just ten minutes and I was moaned at by three teachers for being in the wrong place at the wrong time. I was not making a noise. I was not trying my utmost to destroy the loos. I was just reading alone. Some teachers seem to be rather insincere at times. They do not shout or order me around . . . They are very polite, as if they are just asking me to do something, when I know very well they expect me to do it, no matter how I feel. They smile friendly as if to cover up the fact that they have just given me an order. I will shut up moaning about the teachers in this school because it does not do any good and the more I think about it, the more bitter I feel. Probably if I did not feel so depressed and bored I would see the real goodness there is in some of the teachers.

I feel I need to get away from this place and the people in it because things can only get worse. Probably I am the only person who can twist everything round so that I do know where I am going, yet I do not have the energy. I have got a strange desire to be like a waterfall but I am not alive and fresh enough. I just feel so stale and tired. I want to feel real enthusiasm for something, but there does not seem to be anything. I suppose I have got to search for something. I just do not know. My mind seems to be clogging up so that it is now difficult to really think about anything. Sometimes I feel so lazy and bored I accept what I am told, without a moment's reflection. I am frightened I could be dying as an individual person, with my own life . . .

Spring term, sixth year: February

I am sitting in bed, one minute feeling very depressed and the next minute feeling as though I am really going to live. I have been thinking about when I first came to this school because something which had seemed so full of hope and freshness has disintegrated around me. Perhaps it seems like an exaggeration to most people but that is how I feel. When I first came here I felt frightened because I felt it was a fault in myself that made me dislike my other school. I came here with one thought in my mind: 'If I do not like this school, then there is definitely something wrong in me. The schools are not bad, it is just me.'

The years I spent in the Grammar School were bad for me in several ways but one thing (some people may consider it trivial) which has caused me a lot of confusion is the fact that it was an all-girls' school. If I had been a different sort of person I would not have been affected in the way I was but I was introvert[ed] and lacked confidence. Try to imagine living from the age of 11½ to 14 without speaking to a boy of that age or having any contact with the opposite sex. Probably people will think: 'What do a couple of years matter?' But you see, they matter a great deal, especially at that age when you are developing as a complete individual. If I had made friends out of school perhaps I would not have found things so difficult but I was too shy to go out anywhere, so I stayed indoors, shut away from the realities of life. By not growing up with boys of my age I did not have a chance to understand them. When I was thirteen I still thought of boys as having the same mentality as the boys I knew in my junior school. I came to a stand-still during those years so when I came here I was completely lost. I had forgotten how to live with boys my own age and how to be friends with them. There was no spontaneity. I am just writing about how I was affected because I know that probably only a few are affected as I was.

Before we moved house and I went to the Grammar School, I used to be friends with the boy next door, who was a couple of years older than me. We had been friends for years and while I was at the Grammar School I never saw him, but he was the only boy I could remember ever really knowing and I fretted over him. I suppose people would laugh because of my age but you see, if I had been at a mixed school I would have hardly thought of him, the way I did. When something is missing, it suddenly becomes ridiculously important. There were no boys and it was very unnatural so I had to fill the gap with the only boy who had meant anything to me. Also I knew I would not feel at ease with a boy but I could remember feeling completely at ease with him. He was a scapegoat. Somehow it all seemed unhealthy. It seems so stupid to be cut off from boys like that when you have eventually got to live in a mixed community and possibly marry one. How can you be expected to leave school at eighteen years old and mix naturally, when you have hardly spoken to a boy? How can you cope with emotional problems when you have never had a chance to experience anything on a lighter level? I know this sounds exaggerated and drastic but honestly emotional problems are not all that easy to cope with. Once again I am speaking for myself because I know a lot of people would not get so muddled and confused as me. Being inhibited is a terrible drawback in life . . . I am the sort of person who needs things to be gradual and sure.

I am not really sure why I am writing all this. I suppose I just need to look back on how I have developed and grown up. Really I should not use the term 'grown up' because I have not grown up. Sometimes my emotions run riot with me and then I realise I am not mature enough to cope with my feelings. I have tried but I honestly do not know what to do. I cannot eliminate feelings that are in me, even if I do not want them. I have kept a diary for a long time but for the last four months I have kept an exercise book in which I have recorded my attitudes towards people. I have not written in it every day, just when I have needed to write, and as I read through it now I notice how my feelings about certain people have developed. It has helped me tremendously, because, even though on some days it is obvious I have misunderstood somebody, I can tell by what I write on a later date that I have sorted it all out. I do not try to deliberately connect each piece I write. They are independent, yet time and again I find I have either contradicted myself, or strengthened a point I made earlier. I know people think I am secretive but I just prefer to take my time before I really commit myself. By writing exactly how I feel, I can try to understand myself. Perhaps I sound conceited but I know I am very honest with myself. I cannot pretend to have feelings when I have not. Sometimes I have tried to pretend to feel the opposite to how I do actually feel, but it is useless. Automatically a hidden person in me laughs and says, 'Come off it. You know you do care. Don't try to fool me.' Then I laugh, because it seems so funny to have two people inside me, having such a good-humoured disagreement. The honest person in me always wins which can be painful sometimes.

Writing has helped me a lot because when I was at the grammar school I never used to discuss my feeling or thoughts with anybody, and neither did I write them, so everything got bottled up inside me. The only way I expressed any of my mixed-up feelings was by crying, I always cried, just so that I did not become so full of unexpressed feelings that I exploded.

I think the reason I cannot talk to a lot of people is because I have not got much of a social self. Most people seem to have a social self and a private self, but I seem to be rather lacking in the first. Some people tend to consist mainly of a social self with a very small private self, and this is not particularly satisfactory either . . .

I do not think I accept myself as I am, yet how can I ever expect to be happy when I am dissatisfied so often? I am dissatisfied with this school, so I intend leaving, but I know, as well as everybody else, that this is no solution, because there is nothing real ahead of me. I feel sure a lot of people think I have wasted any intelligence I have, and I can see how they feel, but I am growing up, and I have got to be the one to decide what I do. I am not mature and I will make mistakes but I know if I stay on at school and sit more examinations I will become resentful, blaming other people for the position I am in . . .

Spring term, sixth year: March

I feel disgusted with myself for being the person I have been recently. This time I have really frightened myself because I have just realised the type of person I could always be if I allow myself to remain in this rut . . . Richard, John and David are about the only people who can make me laugh wholeheartedly at myself and that makes me feel better. When I tell my mum about them she thinks I have got a crush on them but she does not know me very well now. I have not got a crush on them. I just feel a strong affection for them, which is love but a certain type of love. They make me feel as though I am smiling inside when we walk through Rosehill Park and they start to have a grass fight. I stand and watch them running about, grass flying everywhere, and I laugh and laugh, everything seems so good and happy. What I feel for them is somewhere deep inside and I cannot explain properly. Sometimes I feel I want to hug them and tell how much they matter to me, but it's just something inside; so I only laugh at their madness. I feel something for Richard but it's a different feeling. Perhaps it's a crush, my mum would think so if I tried to explain why I do not work at school, why I'm moody, etc. I have never felt like this before but the feeling has been in me well over a year so what do I do? I do not know what to do and I realise how much of a child I am. I have wanted him to ask me out all this time but I never forced my company on him because I did not seem to have the right. In some ways I think I'm very prudish. I cannot stand boys kissing me or anything unless I feel a lot for them. As much as I feel for Richard anyway. This probably seems very stupid but that's the way I am. When Richard started kissing me over the park, I suddenly thought, 'I must stop now because to him I could be any girl, while to me, he's him, nobody else.' Afterwards I thought about it and decided I could be wrong so I let it go on. But what's the good of a relationship between 9 a.m. and 3.30 p.m.? Part of the reason I do not do any work is because the only time I see him is at school. All right, so I'm letting myself be carried away by my feelings. I admit that, and I'm totally mixed-up because of it. On Friday he told me he was coming to the barbecue with a girl. He said he was not actually going out with her, his friend had just stopped going out with her and so he was looking after her until she got over it. He asked me if I minded and at first I said what I thought I should feel. 'No I do not mind. I'm not going out with you so it does not matter.' He said, 'That's how it should be,' and I felt horrid. Not really through jealousy this time. I was a bit jealous but it was more because I suddenly felt that all along he had just been playing around and I had not, so I said. 'No, it should not be like that.'

I honestly did not mean to put him in that situation, I did not want to let out [my] bitchiness or anything. I wanted to be sensible but when tears and pain come, I cannot seem to stop them. I think that when I feel hurt I become hard and cold. I should never have got a seventeen year old boy in such a confusion because of how I felt. I cannot cope with my feelings so I should have been more careful with him. What I meant to say, would not come out and I always get mixed-up when I'm upset. I said one of the most selfish and horrid things I could have said to him. I said, 'You don't care a damn about me.' I did not really mean it in that sense because why should he care? I meant, 'Why did not he say he just wanted to have a laugh?' I am over-demanding am I not? I seem to possess all the feelings I despise, like possessiveness and jealousy and look what I have expected of Richard? . . .

Spring term, sixth year: March

I have found the last few months very difficult, and many times I have just wanted to hide away from everything. To crawl into a shell and protect myself from the madness which seemed to surround me. In fact the madness was in me, not around me. Instead of taking a sane look at the way I was feeling I think I must have let myself get caught up in it, because I do not see how I could have got so confused and depressed otherwise. I am not sure why talking to Mr A. made me see most people did accept me, but it did. Perhaps the sun with its warmth and energy is awakening a freshness in me, because I really do feel better. I am growing up and it is so hard. I almost feel a hatred for it, but I think I am probably accepting things better. Myself especially. When I think about the past few months I see I must have developed a rather unhealthy attitude towards people, and, instead of laughing at it, I took it seriously, allowing it the one source of nourishment it needed to grow and grow. Entwining itself round my mind. That was a bad thing for me to do because my mind became imprisoned and any fresh thoughts were forbidden to take root. My mind was unable to search for the sanity it needed in order to heal the pain I had inflicted on myself . . .

Summer term, sixth year: April

I feel stronger now than I have ever felt in the last six years. Perhaps I appear a weak person to a lot of people but, I know, that I am not so weak. I admit I am rather soft and easily hurt but other people cannot sway me when I really believe something. I think I have become stronger because I feel more confident in myself and I think David and Richard have helped me a lot. People have often avoided laughing at me openly, for fear of hurting me, and although at the time I was grateful, I now realise it hindered me because I always took myself and other people seriously. I could never laugh at myself because I felt so self-conscious and inhibited that I could not bear any form of criticism, even if it was only a joke . . . David and Richard have helped me to learn how to laugh at myself because of their warmth and perseverance. When Richard first made jokes about me I felt ever so hurt and confused because I had never been really made fun of before. I used to walk into the classroom and he would call me 'Muscles', making me want to shrivel up to nothing. At the beginning I lost quite a lot of self-confidence and became more inhibited because I felt he must despise me. I really began to feel I must be weird for him to say such mad things. I do not recall feeling so hurt because of David and I think I probably felt at ease with David from the beginning. It is only very recently that I have felt able to talk to Richard, because somehow people who appear very confident in themselves, make me feel uncertain of myself. I used to think I would never feel at ease with Richard but now I can talk to him and I feel grateful to him because I made no effort whatsoever to offer any friendship or warmth. It was not because I did not want to, I just could not but Richard and David really broke through my shell and I am glad they did . . .

Summer term, sixth year: May

I think I must have written all this because I want to know what I have lost in myself which caused me to feel so discontented and restless. Why, when I was younger, could I be content deep inside me, even though there were rules, restrictions and fears? I suppose I accepted everything, whereas now I feel more resentful if anything is forced on me. I cannot feel at peace very often and in a way I am more tense and aggressive. When I say I am more aggressive I do not mean I want to physically fight people, but when people keep bumping into me in the corridor and trivial things like that, I feel more irritated than I should. Sometimes, when I am feeling disgruntled I think, perhaps it is because I find it difficult to accept the fact that I am growing up. If I can tell myself, 'I am never going to be a child again, so I must remember how precious it was, and now I am going to move on,' perhaps I will accept it easier. It is strange that I should find such an inevitable thing hard to accept, but I think I am probably frightened. When I was a child, I could depend on other people whereas now I am more aware of being an individual with my own thoughts. I just want to live my life true to myself and it is not easy.

Catherine's Diary

■ *by Catherine Dunbar* ■

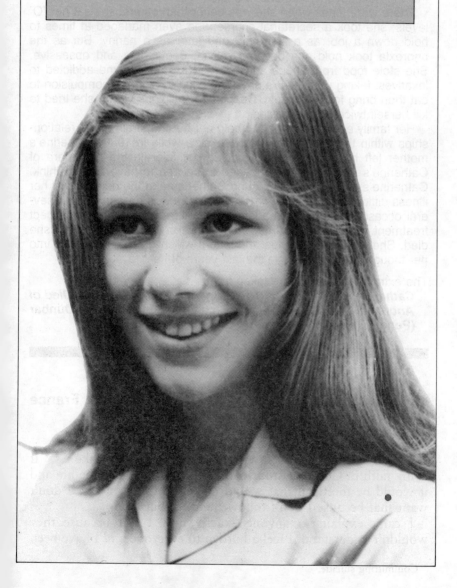

Catherine Dunbar died at the age of twenty-two of anorexia nervosa. She was born in 1962, the third of four children (Simon, Richard and Anna). As a baby, Catherine had had eating difficulties and she had always been finicky about food. In 1976, her father had serious business problems and the family were under a great deal of stress, moving home several times. In the summer of 1976 – with another move imminent – Catherine asked to go to boarding school. In January 1977, Catherine's headmistress rang her mother to say that Catherine had stopped eating. After consultation with a psychiatrist, Catherine was admitted to hospital for the first time. She was then fifteen years old. For the next seven years she struggled with her illness.

There were times when she was better than others: she sat her 'O' levels; she took a secretarial course; she even managed at times to hold down a job, as a secretary and later as a nanny. But as the anorexia took hold she became selfish, demanding and obsessive. She stole food from shops and hoarded it. She became addicted to laxatives, taking up to 140 a day. She used to binge: a compulsion to eat then bring food up again. Despite her religious views, she tried to kill herself twice by overdosing.

Her family and friends tried to help her but the strain made relationships within the family very difficult. For a while in 1980, Catherine's mother left home because she could not tolerate the nightmare of Catherine's illness and she needed to be free to have time to think. Catherine's sister Anna also found Catherine and the demands of her illness difficult to tolerate at times. Catherine was hospitalised on several occasions, sometimes against her will, but she could not accept treatment. She finally returned home and on 2nd January 1984 she died. She left behind diaries and letters which give some insight into her thoughts and feelings in the last years of her life.

The extracts that follow are taken from:
Catherine: A Tragic Life. The Story of a Young Girl who Died of Anorexia Nervosa, written and compiled by Maureen Dunbar (Penguin, 1987)

---

10 March 1978   Amiens, France

(I want to be 6st 7lb [41.4 kg]
   this is a large problem)

I feel fed up and depressed with life sometimes. I feel like c.s.* It is my faith in God that stops me doing it for He gave me life and it would be the devil that would make me take it away. I don't want that because I don't follow the devil but God.

I can't explain to anyone exactly how I feel because they wouldn't understand. I feel a burden to everyone and I have been

---

* Committing suicide.

for a year. I wish to God I didn't feel like this. I'd give anything in the world to be a natural, sane girl, but it doesn't seem meant for me yet. I can't stay here at Amiens as much as I love it, because I am too depressed again and I feel insecure. I am obsessed with my weight, I can't explain fully to Mummy why I want to leave. I can only say my reasons are I'm homesick and disturbed.

I want to take my 'O's in November, and please God I'll succeed at them, if nothing else in life. I just want to hide from people and life and uncertainty. How can I overcome it? It is an impossible task all alone.

Mercredi, 29 mars 1978

I have done so much damage to myself with 3 overdoses (laxatives) in 3 weeks. I am, thank God, 6st 8 at the moment and intend staying like that. I dread to think what comments will be made by people when I don't return to France after Easter but I have decided it's my life and I know what I need. No matter what they say, I shan't let them worry me (I hope). I shall work for my 'O's and afterwards?

January 1980

This morning I got up and tidied the house, then I had a bath and washed my hair. After lunch we went into Marlborough and did the shopping.

We received a letter from Mummy, it was a kindly comforting letter, she has asked that we don't find out where she is. I have tried very hard at lunch and supper to increase my food intake, what will my weight do tomorrow? We took Hugo to the vet this evening. He has now had all his vaccinations. 30.5[kg].

January 1980

Today my weight was 31.00 kilos so I am very tense about it. I have reduced my fluid and food intake today. It has been a funny sort of day, though not as long as I thought it would be. I tidied the house as usual this morning and had a bath. This afternoon I worked at my tapestry and finished typing Simon's notes. Daddy and I went shopping and took Hugo with us in the car. Anna came home this evening, she is very distraught about Mummy and cannot understand why she has left. However by bedtime she seemed all right. I feel very depressed this evening it is a strain for me at present for everyone leans on me and pours out their anxieties and sorrows to me. I have no one with whom I can do this. It is hard. My laxatives have not worked very efficiently today, so that worries me. What will my weight be in the morning? Please dear God may it have dropped or at least not gone up. I can feel the need for a binge building up inside me.

January 1980

My weight was 30.8 this morning which pleased me. It has been a very emotional day though – Grandad died last night. He fell out of bed and had a heart attack.

Oh dear Lord please help us. Mummy is still away – what good is she doing herself? Please help us to get the family reunited very very soon. Amen. May tomorrow bring a ray of hope or light into our lives.

January 1980

My weight was 30.2 kilos today. Quite a drop from yesterday, thank goodness. I felt very relieved and pleased. I didn't swallow very much today and intend keeping my eating down to a minimum now as I want to keep my weight between 30-30.5 kilos. After lunch I drove into Marlborough and back. My driving is very much better today after so much practice yesterday!

Daddy was surprisingly in a bright mood throughout the day, which I never expected at all. Mind you, I think he suffered a slight hangover this morning! We phoned Anna this afternoon, she was very tearful and is pining madly for Mummy to come home.

January 1980

My weight was 30.2 kilos so I felt pleased today. Not an awful lot has happened in fact – I have very little to report. Mummy rang about midday and asked Daddy to collect her. He drove her to London. Apparently, she was very tearful, however she let him take her out to dinner.

I am very depressed. I went on an enormous binge, whilst I was on my own. That didn't please me because I can really manage without that now.

January 1980

...I am in a strange mood, I feel empty and lonely. I don't understand it.

February 1980

I weighed 30 kilos only this morning, that really made my day.

I have been feeling very depressed and ill, my laxatives have made me feel very sick. Daddy left for London at about 4.30 so I then prepared my massive binge which I began at six o'clock and finished at 8.30.

I cleaned the house from top to bottom. I finished typing Simon's notes this morning.

February 1980

My weight was 29.9 kilos today. It will go up again tomorrow because it is just from dehydration after my binge yesterday. I have taken my eating carefully today because I would like to try and keep my weight down tomorrow.

. . . I spoke to Anna on the phone, I think she was a little tearful.

February 1980

My weight was 30 kilos this morning which pleased me, I had expected to jump up more today.

I went on a massive binge which lasted all afternoon. Afterwards I drank 1¼ bottles of soda water, 1 cup of tea and had my usual pick at a Kit-Kat. I also took a suppository and a second dose of laxatives. My stomach feels so bloated even now.

February 1980

I weighed 30.3 kilos this morning, it did not bother me too much as I now realise I must permit myself to fluctuate between 30 and 31 kilos, but I could not bear to be any more than that.

Daddy was really down this morning which made life very dull, dreary, depressing and difficult for me. Anyway, thank God, by the afternoon he had bucked up. I did loads of dictation and typing for him which passed the time.

This evening we both had one hell of a go at one another and were both very irritable.

February 1980

. . . I had a very busy day here, I cleared the house from top to bottom. I actually managed not to binge . . . until supper time, when I went on a long binge. At first it was not very successful but then I carried out a second one and managed to clear my stomach.

February 1980

I weighed 30.1 kilos today, my binge was successful.

I went to London and had my hair cut. I then went to see Mummy, we had a reasonably good talk. I still feel so down because she feels she has made the wrong decision in coming back to Daddy. She is in a low mental state. It really does hurt me deeply . . . I feel numb inside.

February 1980

I weighed 30.4 kilos today. It has been a traumatic day. Daddy left early for London. I just broke down and cried out loud for ages; I can't take any more.

I had an enormous binge this afternoon, basically it is an addiction whenever I am alone in this house. I feel so down.

February 1980
I weighed 30.2 kilos today . . . We met Anna, Mummy and Simon for lunch. Richard had gone to a friend for the day. It was a lovely feeling to be together . . .

This evening we went to Mass at Brompton Oratory and I drove there. Mummy, Daddy and Anna couldn't believe how well I drove!

February 1980
My weight was 30.1 today, I was pleased. I have actually tried to eat a lot more today, so I will have gained weight tomorrow because I always do when I eat even a mouthful more than the previous day.

February 1980
My weight was 30.3 today . . . Daddy was extremely down this morning, but gradually bucked up. He was though, very tense all day. I feel so helpless when he is like this because nothing I do or say will help him.

Anna phoned, she was a little lonely I fear and still feels insecure. Unfortunately I am in a down mood today whereby I am continuously picking at food, so I dread to think what my weight will do tomorrow.

February 1980
I weighed 30.4 today . . . I feel so depressed and low, what is my future? I know that I want, more than anything, to get my secretarial qualifications and begin my career, but at the moment it doesn't look like I shall be able to start again in April, due to the family situation.

I feel everyone dislikes me as a person and I certainly dislike myself. I just pray to God that we can buy the other house and sell this.

I tried harder with my eating today. My laxatives were very effective compared with other days.

February 1980
This morning I weighed 30.5. Daddy was in a really depressed state and I just don't know how I managed to cope with him.

I met Mummy this morning, I love her so much and my love for her today was so strong. I begged her to come back to us.

When I returned home Daddy and I had a row and he just went up to bed saying that he would keep out of my way until Sunday. However that didn't last very long, he came downstairs this evening whilst I was binging. Anyway he didn't notice, so I just disappeared upstairs.

We made it up when I came down.

4 March 1980

My weight was 30.2 kilos this morning so I was really pleased, although I do now realise that the time has come when I really must put on some weight, particularly as we have sold the house and that means that we will be moving in under a fortnight. The day for exchanging contracts is this Friday.

I ate a lot more today.

5 March 1980

I now weigh 30.5 kilos. I know that I must let my weight rise, but I am scared to do so. However I feel too thin the way I am. I want to be able to wear nice clothes again. I know that I will feel better and more normal in every sense if I could put on some weight. I long to feel as a girl of my age should feel.

I took Mummy the contract to sign for the house today. I hope she decides to come back to the family. I think that she will.

March 1980

I weighed 30.9 kilos. I went to see Mummy this morning and she has told me that she is coming back to us, I am just so thrilled. She would like me to go to France with her and Anna on the 31st. I will wait and see.

March 1980

I weighed 30.9 kilos this morning. We left home at seven and spent the whole day in Surrey seeing builders, etc.

There is just so much to do that I feel quite depressed. Will we ever move and *get* settled again? I drove round all the old haunts and they just bring back so many memories. I long to move back there again – I really do.

April 1980

I weighed 31.9 today . . . I felt in complete control after my binge today as I saw myself in the mirror – a skeleton.

April 1980

This morning I weighed 31.5 kilos. Anna gave me a real talking to about my anorexia and asked me what I was going to do about it. To be honest, I don't really know.

April 1980

This morning I could not weigh myself as Anna hid the weighing scales from me. I was panicking as I am sure I have put on some weight. However I have so far taken two lots of laxatives and shall take some more this evening after supper . . .

Mummy came round at lunch time and Daddy took her out. They went to Croydon.

I went to see Mr – at Nestlé's. He was very nice, I have been offered the job and accepted it. I begin on Monday.

August 1980
I have never felt as ill and weak today since last November. How I survived work I will never know.

25 June 1981
Mood: Mixed
Weight: 31.2 kilos
Breakfast: Tea. Kit-Kat
Lunch: Tea, soda-water, Kit-Kat, 2 cinnamon danish, 1 cheese
Supper: 2 rolls, cheese dish, 1 Kit-Kat, tea
Binge: Bread, crisps, popcorn, swiss rolls, sugar puffs, remainder of supper cheese dish.
Laxatives: 105 this morning and evening (work)
Remarks: Not too bad a day. Gilly and Anna finished their 'O' levels and came home. Daddy not really speaking to me. I binged because I just felt obsessional.

26 June 1981
Mood: Abnormally cheerful
Weight: 31.1
Breakfast: Kit-Kat and tea
Lunch: Tea, soda water, Kit-Kat, 2 cinnamon, 1 cheese.
Supper: Tea, Kit-Kat, 2 sausage rolls, spring greens, mashed potato (knowing I could binge later).
Binge: Spring greens, sausage rolls, potatoes (boiled and mashed), toast, apple pickings, cottage chese pickings, shreddies.
Laxatives: 109 approx. morning and evening (work)
Remarks: Not too bad a day. I knew the family would be going out this evening about 9 o'clock so I had supper about 7.50 and then binged later when they were out. I felt quite cheerful today but deep down I feel a wave of depression and am waiting for it to break out. It could be a few days, one can never tell with me.

28 June 1981
Mood: Depressed
Weight: 30.4
Breakfast: 1½ Kit-Kats, tea.
Lunch: Cornish pasty, 2 sausage rolls, cheese dish, tea, 1½ Kit-Kats.
Supper: Roast beef, cabbage, boiled new potatoes, Yorkshire pudding, gooseberry fool and 1½ Kit-Kats, tea.
Binge: I began at 4.00 and finished 7.30. Bread, sausages, cheese, sugar puffs, sweets, bonbons then a second one on Twiglets, cheese puffs, sweets and crisps.
Laxatives: 145 approx. 5l this morning, 9 3/4 evening 7.30.

Remarks: This morning I really broke down and sobbed my heart out to Mummy and Daddy. I have just given up hope of ever getting better. Mummy, I am sure, is the only person who can help me. I had a dreadful afternoon binging and I have no idea how much food I retained in me, but it feels a lot. I weighed 31.00 kilos after it. It is now 11.30 and the extra laxatives are not having much effect. My stomach is bloated and full of wind. May I have not gained tomorrow. I am so scared and mentally torn inside. Dear Jesus, please help me.

7 July 1981
Mood: Mixed. High/Low
Weight: 30.2
Breakfast: 1½ Kit-Kats, tea.
Lunch: 1½ Kit-Kats, tea, soda water, 3 cinnamon.
Supper: 1 sausage roll, 1 pasty, potatoes, cheese dish, tea.
Binge: Supper incorporated, 2 boiled eggs, bread, Dutch crisp bakes, mousaka, cereal, 2nd mousaka, potatoes, Dutch crisp bakes, bread, sweets.
Laxatives: 110 approx.
Remarks: My binging went on the whole evening and when Mummy and Daddy arrived home I still had not finished. I don't feel that I managed to get it all up. Hence, what will my weight do tomorrow?

23 July 1981
Mood: Fair
Weight: 31.4
Breakfast: 1 Kit-Kat, tea
Lunch: 2 cinnamon, 2 cheese, Kit-Kat, Fresca, tea.
Supper: 3 sausage rolls, cheese dish, Kit-Kat, tea.
Binge: Marmite and mustard on rye bread, French toasts, Frosties.
Laxatives: 115 approx
Remarks: Daddy was away tonight. I binged, am feeling low but cannot cry to ease it.

Monday, 4 January 1982
I woke up at 6.15 and went through my normal ritual of getting up, having my breakfast and reading the paper. I was really prepared to go into hospital today, I had got everything ready and everyone has been so fantastic in helping me prepare for it. I am so scared tonight because I did not go and have lost my nerve for going in. If only I could have smoked, but I couldn't possibly have given that up as well as my laxatives, Kit-Kats,

routine and freedom. Worst of all I know deep down that I will never be able to eat or face gaining weight, but at least had I gone, I would have felt I had given it a try. I can just see how everything is going to go now. Daddy will never smile or do anything to please me. He will pressurise me and I cannot face that. If only he would understand that it really is not my choice that I should die, but that I am trapped. In the forefront of my mind is the fact that I know I can never eat and gain weight. I am just fooling myself.

I feel so selfish after all that has been done for me. I will now take a back seat and live in my room, taking my tea to my room and not cooking supper. I do not want to be a burden or an irritation to anyone anymore; besides I have caused many problems in the past and am causing more now. If I keep out of the way the better it will be for all concerned. I have decided to cut down on my intake of food, not that that is very possible as I eat so little anyway.

I just pray that I do not live for another two months but die very soon. I know I am a selfish person at present and a big coward. The sooner I go the better. I cannot face the guilt that I feel at the moment. I was prepared to go into Barts, I really was and when I have my mind made up to do something and things don't go that way, it is just too much. For the first time ever today I realised death is inevitable. I feel helpless and trapped.

Wednesday, 6 January 1982
I woke up with a start at 7.15 and rushed downstairs because I thought that my breakfast might clash with Daddy leaving for work. I received a 'thank-you' letter from Granny. I feel terrible because I just cannot write to anyone at present. I have lost my concentration. My mind feels numb and today I felt like a rag doll that had lost its stuffing. I cannot cope with the change in my regime. I know in my heart of hearts that I will die. Hospital will do no good, I cannot bear to leave home. I just pray that I am left in peace to die. I want no more pressures from anyone, it puts me in a state of turmoil so that I don't know where to turn.

Saturday, 16 January 1982
Today was one of my worst days for a long time. This morning I went into Croydon, Mummy drove me. I bought a bath robe and some magazines and then I came home. This outing unsettled me because it is not usual. This afternoon I was in mental agony. I just felt like eating and binging. Binging is the only way I have of remaining in my own world and of being able to indulge in food, thus taking my mind off everything, particularly my problems. Vomiting uses up my mental and physical energy, sometimes

it leaves me hyperactive, but today it left me feeling drowsy. I am so restless and unhappy I cannot go on. I don't know what will happen, I just know that I cannot face hospital.

Wednesday, 27 January 1982
I have never felt so low and depressed as I did today. I feel so trapped. I want to live for my family's sake but I cannot live with myself. Anna was so sweet this evening, she came and sat next to me and just hugged me, this helped me. Daddy was so sweet too and Mummy as always, a tower of strength. Father Taggart came today and gave me Holy Communion.

I keep waking up at night – I have these bad dreams of intruders in the house.

Oh I do need help and love at home, and I get it, but I cannot help feeling very low.

Sunday, 31 January 1982
... Anna was so sweet and said 'don't worry Catherine, you cannot help getting like this'. I told Richard how I love him even though I may not show it. I have been wanting to say that to him for a long time now.

Friday, 5 February 1982
... I cried to Anna when she came in. Simon and Jenny came and brought me the most beautiful bunch of flowers, these gestures mean more than anything to me.

Wednesday, 11 February 1982
... Oh Jesus help me, I can do nothing. I am worn out with life. Please do things for me your way.

Monday, 21 February 1982
With Daddy away I am able to lie in all this week. I felt quite chirpy this morning because I always look forward to being able to talk to Dr Foot, I find it such a relief. She examined my heart today, it is the same as before. It amazes me that I am still alive because by looking at me medically speaking it would seem impossible for my body to tick over. She says that it is a question of mind over body. The fact that I still have hope that I will miraculously be able to face treatment one day is evidently what is keeping me alive. She gave me a prescription for some antidepressants ...

Monday, 1 March 1982
I was feeling very depressed today. When Dr Foot came I just wanted to break down and cry. I just couldn't open up and talk. When she had gone, I so wanted her to come back so that I could unburden myself to her ... I know I won't die yet, I just know it and I really do want to so very much now. I cannot face hospital

but how much longer am I going to go on living this type of existence? I can't bear it; I had a long chat with Mummy after lunch. It eased me a little. This evening I just locked myself away and binged. I weighed 26.9 afterwards and finished at approx. 12.30 a.m. I eventually got into bed at about 1.30.

Monday, 5 April 1982
I arrived at St Antony's Hospital with Mummy and Daddy at about 2.45 p.m. We had a very warm welcome, and it really is a lovely place. I have my own room with a shower and toilet en suite, remote-control colour TV, radio and an electronic bed. The staff are very kind and warm. I don't feel institutionalised or as though I am in hospital. For supper I had fried fillet of plaice and mixed vegetables followed by cheese and biscuits and a cup of tea with my Kit-Kat. Mummy, Richard and Anna came this evening. At 9 p.m. I had some Bovril, then at 9.30 I had 2 Kit-Kats and cup of tea. I had a bath and then just pottered around before I went to bed. The doctor came to see me at 7.30 and made me feel very relaxed. He prescribed some Valium for me and some other tablets. He is going to have me connected to a cardiac machine tomorrow also, I am to have several other tests carried out. At 3.30 p.m., 1¾ after my lunch, I weighed in at 27.2 kilos.

Thursday, 6 May 1982
I woke up after a not too good night's sleep. Everything went according to schedule this morning. The doctor came in at 10.00 and we chatted about tube feeding. I felt very calm and placid this morning. In my own mind I know I will never eat without help and that therefore tube feeding is the only way I will survive, but it will be another week or two before I can begin. I know that I can only accept it when I feel ready. I told the doctor this. He said my heart would probably be all right while I sat here. He is concerned about the electrolyte system in my body. I really got into my knitting before lunch. Lunch was late and I felt myself getting really agitated. After lunch I was all shaky and zombie-like, my speech was slurred . . . I cannot give . . . a date on which I will start tube feeding. I reckon it will be 2–3 weeks, at least, but it is better that way, than before I am ready. It is my mental state. I actually can feel my body packing up now. I know in myself that time is running out.

Wednesday, 12 May 1982
Once again I am writing my diary, it has been a few days since I last wrote it, but I have been so depressed. I will not die, but just sit here getting no better until the money runs out. I look back and see just how little progress I have made and can never go home until I am well. I have asked Mummy to telephone the

doctor and explain to him exactly how I feel, before I see him tomorrow. I just don't know what to do or where to turn any more. I can't open the door to life . . .

26 February 1983
Right now, I feel lost, lonely and frightened. I cannot cope with my binging here. I cannot stay, my anorexia takes even more of a hold on me when away from Mummy. I will not accept any form of treatment, but I do know for certain that without Mummy I am just totally unable to cope. I realise the situation at home but I feel that Anna is being a little hard on me. I have to come home to live right now. I just don't know what will happen to me. I love my father and all my family but I need even more my mother. I need her to keep me as sane as I will ever be. I have so much hidden inside myself, I need to be near her, WITH HER. Is that fair? I ask myself. Well at this moment in time, I just know that I need her more so than even Anna. Anna is strong, intelligent and sensible, but me, I have no confidence and am just a little helpless baby. All I can do is cry and cry Help me, save me, help me please. At least Mummy rescue me. I know what its like when Anna and I are together but right now I am in pieces. I dread and fear Daddy's reaction, his fury, frustration and anger because of my inability to be away from Mummy. But sometimes Anna has got to be made to understand . . . I could fill this whole book with talk. But basically it is all a vicious circle. I need my mother, my home, my room and all my things to keep me alive. I can no longer eat anything just drink coffee, bovril and suck lemon ice cubes. It is not a threat but I am so choked I just cannot carry on. I will never be able to work again. I shall just be lonesome invalid who lives in her world, with room for my mother. I just don't know where to turn or what to do or say. God please take me. Having to go away and be away has made me realise just exactly who and what I am. Hard, it may seem to believe, but believe me it has cut me up completely.

The following morning
This morning I feel so frightened and alone, I just want to sit and cry. I need my home and Mummy. Oh God where do I go? I cannot face up to it, life I mean like this. I need my home, my room, my family, but more than anything in this world I need Mummy. I feel so awful after binging last night, I weigh one kilo more today. Oh where am I wanted, where can I go where I will feel secure if I can't go home? I think Anna should have to accept me, for surely I have the right to be at home. If she chooses to give up because of me then I cannot help that. I am who I am. She is intelligent and strong willed, surely she can try to be logical but she just seems to work herself into a state.

GOD I'M HUMAN AND HELPLESS
JUST HELP I CANNOT GO ON
AWAY FROM MUMMY SAVE ME, HELP
MUMMY YOU ARE MY SAVIOUR MY LIFE
I CANNOT LIVE WITHOUT YOU.

You have to see and understand this. I cannot possibly live like this away from you. Help please help say you want me.

I know I am a burden, trouble, a pain. But the pain which is going through me all the time is just too great to explain. All I know is it hurts. Please stay with me, help me. Just being with you, knowing you are always by my side is what helps me. It may not seem that way, but yesterday and the past few days have all been too great. No one has really thought of some way to a solution because it is a question of just getting me away but you can't just do that, I can't take it. I just can't. I wish I could explain how I feel but nothing I say is ever taken seriously, it is always one big vicious circle.

'Since 18 you have had your own way' TRUE TRUE but no one can make me better – I just need love and Mummy. I love Daddy too very very much, don't think that I don't, but everyone is different. Help me, be near me by me stand with me. The agony I am in is too great. I wish for all our sakes God would take me. That is why I am now on a total starvation diet. In fact I am so choked up and filled with pain that I don't even feel like eating. But then at night when I am scared and alone I binge because of the thought of being without Mummy and home.

It is a way of trying to numb my pain and torture myself. Oh I don't know where to stop. Hurry, hurry, take me in your arms and never let me go. Please never let me go. I will die I am cut into pieces so small that I can never put them together again. Oh if only you and Anna could understand this, if I could, if Daddy, Simon, Richard, Jenny or anyone could. I am just a baby. I can't live or fend for myself by myself.

HELP
COME TO ME PLEASE

Every car I hear I hope it is you but time drags and I am scared that you won't come.

Daddy Mummy the world there is no solution to my problem. Just I need home and you. You cannot just write me off until June or for a minute. If you didn't want me why did you bring me into this world.

I am on a knife's edge and can't help any more.

This is no business problem but a problem (what sort you would call it I don't know).

Oh are you coming to help me, I am just like a new-born infant
but with more feeling and fear and loneliness.

HELP   HELP   HELP

Stay with me help
me please help
stay, stay, stay hold
me show me you love
me despite my horrid personality and
what I appear to be.
But I am alive and Oh God here goes
what more can I say it just goes
on and on. It never ends Take me
I would rather you killed me than leave me
I seriously mean it. Stay with me
take me back to my home
my land of living I cannot cope with different places

HELP   PLEASE   PLEASE

take me. I'm alone so alone I am not
normal I am odd so it is so easy for you
to say a day or two won't give it a try
but for me it is a lifetime of misery
and every second is at least a year. Come
Come my God don't think that I don't
care about Anna because I do very much
and even now if she fails I shall be at
fault and carry that burden too
But I am just being destroyed we have
to find a solution you cannot just say
do this you're going there, it's tough
because it isn't right I'm not able
to really explain how I feel because there is
no way in which I can do so.
It's easy for you humans to be logical
and try to explain that what is happening
is right because I am so odd

Call it what you like. But help please
    please just help me.

RIGHT NOW Take me home, let's take
it from there but I cannot stay here away
from you.

The Diary of a Teenage Health Freak

■ *by 'Pete Payne'* ■

Fourteen-year-old Pete Payne is a character created by Ann McPherson and Aidan Macfarlane. They are both doctors who wanted to write a book about teenage health problems. They thought it would be more interesting and fun if it was written as if it were the diary of a typical teenager.

The extracts that follow are taken from:
   The Diary of a Teenage Health Freak, **Aidan Macfarlane and Ann McPherson (Oxford University Press, 1987)**

About this diary's writer

GENERAL INFORMATION

Name   Peter H. (daren't tell you the rest) Payne.
Nickname   'Know it All Pete'.
Date of birth   17 December 1972.
Age   14 Years and 1 month.
Born   according to Mum, half-way down the corridor at the hospital, on the way to the labour room.
Address   18 Clifton Road, Hawsley, London.
Hobbies   picking my nose, watching telly, worrying about myself, teasing my younger sister, annoying people by being a 'know all', collecting medical facts, reading photographic magazines, having accidents.
Heroes   John Lennon, myself, Sam's dad, Adrian Mole, whoever it was discovered penicillin but I can't remember, Marilyn Monroe.
What I'll be when I grow up   myself, a famous scientist, very rich, and very very attractive to girls.
Personality   shy, awkward, unattractive to girls, afraid of life, shirker at washing up, tease (especially of Susie), bad at sport; but enjoy helping old ladies cross roads, doing my homework before watching telly (except when *Match of the Day* is on), making witty comments and being original.
Worries   catching AIDS, growing up and being unemployed.

PHYSICAL MAKE UP

Sex   male and becoming more so.
Height   five feet and four inches against my doorpost using Mum's measuring tape.
Weight   58 kilos but ate a big supper.
Hair   colour brown.
Eye colour   brown to match.

Distinguishing marks   the whole of me but especially the brown birthmark on my bum.

MY MOTHER

Name   Jane Elspeth Margret.
Date of birth   June 1945 but can't remember date.
Age   35 for the last six years.
Job   part-time in building society, cook, cleaner, clothes washer, general neighbourhood 'do gooder', doctor to all of us, looking after Dad, worrying about us all.
Weight   chubby.
Hair   colour brown.
Eye   colour green with flecks.
Distinguishing marks   her laugh, like a sick hyena.
Personality   noses into my private life all the time, makes me be nice to stupid relations, doesn't take any notice when I have sleeping problems etc. and just says 'you'll get over it', is always saying 'have you done your homework', but is cuddly, a good listener, and doesn't bother me about my room the way Sam's mum does.

MY FATHER

Name   Anthony Tobias.
Date of birth   don't know.
Age   nobody knows.
Job   kills tiny beasties in people's houses. It's called 'pest control' which is what I do to my sister Susie.
Weight   expanding.
Hair   receding – what's left of it.
Eye colour   can't remember.
Distinguishing marks   awful moustache.
Personality   funny, good mechanic, won't stop smoking secretly, always talking politics, knows about a lot of things.

MY OLDER SISTER

Name   Sally (and Beatrix – Top Secret).
Date of birth   keep forgetting.
Age   17.
Weight   a state secret.
Hair colour   changes all the time.
Eye colour   blue.
Personality   worse 'know all' than me, bossy, and will do almost anything for money which she's saving up to buy a motorbike with.

MY YOUNGER SISTER

Name Susie Jane (lucky her – they'd run out of awful names).
Date of birth tells us about six times a day – 14 January 1974.
Age 12 years and 11 months.
Hair colour mousy.
Eye colour mousy too – like the rest of her.
Distinguishing marks none.
Personality worries about what her friends will think of her
    family, enjoys shopping, giggles, doesn't obey my orders, and
    overreacts on purpose when I tell her off, especially if Mum's
    around.

MY BROTHER

Unfortunately Mum and Dad never gave me one.

MY BEST FRIEND

Name Sam Sproggs.
Sex says he's male.
Age claims he's 14. Most of the time behaves like he's 4.
Personality crazy about bicycles, attractive to girls but ignores
    them, tries to be original but isn't, gets more pockets money
    than me.

ROMANTIC ATTACHMENTS

Name Cilla Jeffs.
Sex yes, if she'll let me.
Age 14.
Where she lives not saying.
Why I like her just do.

PETS

Type cat (Sally's) which would starve to death if Mum didn't
    feed her.
Name Bovril.
Age 14 demented months and losing all her hair.

MY HOUSE

Semi-detached with more bays than the South Coast. Metal round
the windows like every other house for miles around. Three bed-
rooms and a shoe-box for Susie. Pink tiles in the bathroom. Fitted
carpets everywhere. Hairs on Mum's suite where the cat's been.
Kitchen fixtures care of Dad, so not quite finished yet.

MY ROOM

'IN and OUT' message board on the outside of the door, and paper skeleton on the inside. Bed with all my old clothes down the back. Paddington Bear one million times over on my bedcover. Dad's yellow paint over bumpy wallpaper, picture of aeroplane by me, covered with Marilyn Monroe 'on the grating' poster. Books everywhere ranging from Biggles to Asimov.

Tuesday 19 February

Mum and Dad getting at one another again this evening. Sally made it worse by saying she was going to be out late. Mum said she should ask, not tell, and what about the revision for her 'A' levels? Sally flounced out saying that all her friends were allowed to stay out late, even on weekdays. Her parting shot was that she was not only old enough to get married, but also old enough to have a baby. Could see that shook Mum rigid. Beat a hasty retreat to my diary. Heard Sally coming in early, slamming the front door meaningfully. Seems that Mum's got more control over Sally than over Bovril, the cat, who's out all night waking the neighbourhood with her sex life.

Wednesday 20th February

Worried as woke with a headache again. In such a state nearly mistook Mum's sleeping tablets for paracetamol, and forgot my maths book. Was late meeting Sam who was furious. Both late for school. Sam disappeared with other friends at break, and I had no one to talk to. Finally had to stay on for my detention. Not only bored with all my work at school but couldn't even be bothered with my homework.

Thursday 21st February

Sally spent hours in the bathroom tarting herself up for Mike, her latest boyfriend, while everyone else hung around waiting. Susie's been moaning about having no friends. Kate's gone off and found a new best friend – don't blame her. Susie yelled at me for not passing the sugar. She's too fat to have it anyway. Turns out Jane's asked Sam to the cinema on Friday, and what's more he's going. Thought I was going with him. He seems to like Jane more than me and, much as I want to, I'm too shy to ask Cilla. Maybe I'm gay because I'd rather go with Sam.

Friday 22nd February

Pouring with rain – got soaked going to school. Both Mum and my maths teacher asked me if I had got out of bed the wrong side. Felt exhausted and had a headache all day, and was still fed up with the idea of not going to the film.

Then came the BIG bust up. Real Clint Eastwood style on a domestic scale. I spilt some tea by mistake. Susie said it was on purpose because it was her turn to clear and wash up, and that I had to wipe it up. Didn't see why I should as it was HER turn. She made a face and stomped to the kitchen with a pile of dishes. So I spilt her tea, and when she came back told her now she had something of her own to clear up. She tried to hit me. I caught and twisted her arm. She fell and hit the table and the milk bottle fell and smashed on the floor. At this point Mum reappeared looking as black as thunder. Told her it was all Susie's fault and Susie, lying as usual, said it was all mine. Mum threw a washing-up cloth at Susie and a brush at me, telling us to get on with clearing it up. Then she walked out in a real bate.

Immediately Susie slopped milk all over my new trainers, whispering, 'I hate you', so told her she was a real pain and no wonder Kate didn't like her any more. As I said it, I was aware, with terrible certainty and delighted fear, that it would provoke violence. She hit me on the arm with her milk-sodden tea towel, so I screamed and collapsed (unhurt) on the floor clutching my arm, accidentally cutting myself on the broken glass on the floor. At that instant both Mum and Dad appeared – Mum at one door speechless with rage, and Dad at the other, fresh from beastie bashing, equally speechless. Mum recovered first, yelling, 'BOTH TO BED – NOW'. Dad blurted out, 'Do what your mother says.' I cried, 'But I'm bleeding', and Susie said, 'But it was all his fault, why do you always pick on ME?' 'BED,' Mum screamed, so, deliberately dripping blood all up the stairs, stamped up to my room, slamming the door. Lay listening to Susie sobbing. Maybe 'feeling fed up' is infectious.

What seemed hours later, Sally came up to fetch us for supper. In Susie's room the sobbing immediately began again, followed by a shout of 'No – leave me alone, everybody hates me.' In my worst whiney voice I recited as loud as I could:

'Nobody likes me, everybody hates me,
Think I'll eat some worms.
Big fat juicy ones,
Slip slap slimy ones,
Watch them squiggle and squirm.
Bite their heads off,
Suck their guts out,
Throw their skins away.
Everybody wonders why I live on three fat worms a day.'

Sally shouted at me to shut up. When I stopped I heard her say, much to my surprise, 'No they don't hate you. We all love you very much, including Pete.' Lies, lies, lies.

Supper was a dead silent affair. Had neither the energy nor the nerve to reject my beans and kidneys – even though I didn't feel hungry. Dad made one or two of his feeble jokes which disappeared into the generally shitty atmosphere without a ripple. Came straight up after supper to write this. Sometimes writing about things seems to make them better.

10 p.m. Thought I had finished for the day – but couldn't sleep for Mum and Dad shouting at one another and the throbbing of my cut. The argument seemed to start again with something about Gran coming on holiday, but the battlefield soon broadened to become more bloody and make less sense than even Susie and me.

It appeared Dad never gave Mum any support looking after us, never did any cooking, washing up or cleaning, always forgot her birthday and for that matter Valentine's Day, never fed the cat, never washed the bath after himself, spent the whole of some nights with a headache, never wiped his feet, always left oily bits of the car all over the sitting room sofa, and was always indulging our materialistic needs and never considering hers. Dad, in Mum's pauses, claimed that she always left the car with no petrol in, was illogical, never appreciated the fact that he came shopping with her, always got the pages of the newspaper muddled up, never put the top back on the toothpaste and, worst of all, us children were becoming just like her . . . and so it went on.

Suddenly felt absolutely miserable and really worried. Did this mean that Mum and Dad were going to get divorced? It would be all my fault. I had, I had to admit, started it all, when I was feeling fed up. If Mum and Dad separated life wouldn't be worth living. I wasn't tired any more. I had to talk to somebody, anybody, about it all. I crept along to Susie's room but she wasn't there, so tried Sally's and there were Sally and Susie curled up in bed together chatting. I collapsed on the floor with a sigh, aware of the silence that had descended downstairs.

Sally whispered, 'Don't worry, it's not yours or Susie's fault. Grown-ups often have rows. I'm amazed you haven't heard Mum and Dad before. You two don't have the monopoly on quarrels you know. An occasional row is a normal part of life and it doesn't necessarily mean that the people don't like each other. You have to know and understand someone really well to be able to love them, help them and be nice to them, and to know how to hurt them too! Mike and I have terrible rows sometimes, and they often seem to be about the silliest things. But I do think it's better than bottling things all up, like Uncle Bob and Aunt Pam have been doing for the last twenty-five years. There's nothing like a good row for clearing the air. You wait and see tomorrow.' Tried telling Sally how awful I felt, and she really seemed to know what I meant. She even put a plaster on my cut.

Monday 25th February

Nothing much happened on Sunday, but at school today a group of my friends were discussing parents. Mat's parents are divorced. They had terrible rows all the time, threw things at one another, and then when his dad finally left, no one told him the truth – his mum just said that he'd gone off for a holiday. This scared me, but it sounded much worse than Mum and Dad. Mat said that even if he wished his mum and dad were still together, it was more peaceful now. When I got home, Sally had left one of her magazines on my bed. It had an article by some child psychiatrist about teenagers feeling depressed.

MOODS AND DEPRESSION IN TEENAGERS

Sometimes it is difficult to tell the difference between being fed up and being depressed. One tends to merge with the other. Some people see being depressed as being very, very fed up. However, we all feel fed up sometimes, and perhaps even occasionally a bit depressed. Luckily few of us suffer from severe depression. Many of the things which make us moody can seem much worse, and indeed almost insurmountable, if we are already depressed.

Listed below are some of the things which may cause you to feel this way.
- feeling very unsure of yourself.
- loss, separation or rejection, for example, death or rejection by a loved relative, boyfriend or girlfriend.
- separation or divorce of parents.
- family conflicts.
- feelings of inability to cope.
- depression in one's own parents.
- serious illness.
- alcoholism or drug abuse.
- problems in relationships with friends.
- overly high parental expectations.
- work problems.

If several of these problems occur together, you may feel it is impossible to cope and even wonder whether it is worth while going on living. If this happens, help and treatment are available. It's much better to try and talk to somebody about it rather than keep it all to yourself. The best person is somebody YOU find it easiest to talk to. It may be your best friend, your mother or father, sister or brother, teacher, doctor, priest or vicar, aunt, friend.

It is sometimes difficult to recognise exactly when being fed up becomes being depressed, but this list might help:
- feelings of complete hopelessness and helplessness.
- feeling that everything in the future is going to be bad.
- feeling that the smallest task is impossible.
- being very self-critical over a long time, so that you think nothing you do is ever any good.
- feelings of continued tiredness over days or weeks.

- being unable to sleep for many nights on end, and waking up early in the morning when this is not normal for you.
- frequent headaches and/or tummy pains for which there is no obvious cause.
- loss of appetite with loss of weight, or compulsive eating.
- feelings of being cut off from everyone around you, including family and friends.
- work suddenly seems much more difficult to do.
- staying away from school or running away from home.

None of these things by themselves, or just lasting for a few hours, or a day, mean you are seriously depressed. However, it is when one or more of them occur over several weeks that this may be depression and you should then get help. It is not nice being depressed. It is like an illness and needs to be treated.

Saturday 16th March

A real find – but I hope nobody reads THIS! Susie's out this morning buying new clothes again with Mum, after moaning about wearing Sally's cast-offs. All she wants these days is to be trendy like her friends. Was desperately looking for my only clean T-shirt, mottoed 'let us grow up, not blow up'. All my others were dirty and stuffed down the side of my bed as I had as usual forgotten to give them to Mum to wash. Eventually found it in Susie's bottom drawer, PLUS HER DIARY! Didn't mean to read it but it just sort of fell open in my hands.

Tuesday 26th February

At school today Dave, a real creep who wears flares, asked Kate if she'd started yet. She went red and said no and it was none of his business anyway. Later told me she had and that was why she wouldn't go swimming with me last week. Was really miffed that she hadn't told me before. They started two months ago. She had been staying at her gran's and had had a tummy ache and gone to bed early. In the morning she'd woken up and thought that she'd wet the bed. But it was just a little blood. She'd felt very embarrassed and didn't know what to do with the sheets, but her gran was really nice. Kate said her mum had told her all about it and she had wanted to start her periods, but now she had, she felt a bit annoyed. Though she was also glad to have joined the other girls who had started in the same year. This definitely made ME feel left out. Anyhow her gran had bought some towels as she didn't have any in the house – her periods had stopped years ago. Her gran had said that when she was young nobody had told her anything. They called periods the 'curse' and their 'monthlies' and thought they were dirty, and for some reason when they had one weren't even allowed to wash their hair. She had had to wear an awful elastic belt thing to keep a thick towel in place, which felt a bit like wearing a mattress; but luckily she knew that today they have very comfortable, slim 'press on' ones – the very latest style. Kate's mum had also told her about tampons, and said that it would be perfectly

OK to use them, especially if she wanted to go swimming, but Kate wasn't sure she wanted to try them yet.

Kate's lent me a book her mum had got her, called Have You Started Yet? *It's good and has lots of people's points of view in it, and tells you in a simple way exactly what happens and how. I think I might get embarrassed discussing periods, but reading about them is fine. I don't know what it'll be like for me. I'm not really scared. I suppose it's just part of growing up. It's funny to think that some of my friends can have babies already. Really strange.*

Couldn't find my new pink socks this evening.

Sunday 17th March

Have to be careful what I say in front of Susie or she'll wonder how I know, but I'm glad I don't have periods. Wish that my voice breaking just happened like that though, overnight. For months now when I open my mouth I'm not sure what's going to come out, a foghorn or a squeak. My changes must be obvious to everyone because Dad keeps trying to bring up the subject of puberty and 'the facts of life'. Must have been him that left the book about sex and puberty in my room. This morning he started to tell me about what he called 'the birds and the bees', so I informed him I knew it all already – to help him out, as I began to feel as embarrassed as he seemed. He looked relieved and rushed off to the garage. I really feel for Dad sometimes. I wonder if Mum's behind all this concern? I'd have thought she had enough to worry about with Susie's changes. Don't know why grown-ups want to talk about those things all the time. Think Mum and Dad must be obsessed with sex.

Thursday 28th March

Feeling bored. Tried to find Susie's diary again. It's not there. Has she guessed? Knowing her, she's probably dusted it for fingerprints.

Friday 29th March

Discovered! After school Susie disappeared. At supper she gave us all meaningful looks and announced she'd bought a diary with a lock on. Mum suggested she could look after the spare key if Susie wanted, and then suddenly went bright red.

Saturday 30th March

Have taken to hiding MY diary under my mattress.

Tuesday 9th April

Spent Easter with Sam's family in Wales. Forgot to take my diary as it was under my mattress.

Monday 15th April

Back to school. Whole world suddenly sex obsessed, though at school it's called 'Life Changes' or 'Personal Guidance' or 'Human

Reproduction'. Had a 'Now no sniggering while I put this on the blackboard' class today, all about the physical facts.

Boys' puberty tends to start between the ages of ten and thirteen, and finishes at any time up to eighteen. There's still time for me then, as I'm shorter than many of my friends. Even the girls are taller, but apparently on average they start their changes two years ahead of us boys.

In boys, the first thing is our balls get bigger, and over three years they increase seven times in size. Next comes pubic hair, and bits of hair under our arms, and with some of us hair on our chests too. Hope I don't get hair on my chest. Nothing much I can do about it if I do. Wonder if anyone shaves there? Then our height goes shooting up – can't be too soon for me. We grow a quarter of our final height during this time. Finally our penis grows in length. All these things start at different times in different boys, go on for different lengths of time, and occur in different orders. In one way, we all end up the same after we've been through puberty, but also we all end up different, because we still have different sizes and shapes and looks.

Lots of other changes are going on too. Our muscles are getting bigger and heavier, our shoulders broader, our voices deeper. This is something to do with bigger vocal cords. Like Susie's changes, all these things in boys are controlled by chemicals called hormones produced in the brain.

Wednesday 12th June

Feeling hard done by the last few days. My mates have all gone on a school field trip to Cornwall. Only twenty places and I wasn't given one of them. We're having to WORK while they're having a good time, and we're being taught by real wet teachers while all the good ones are off enjoying themselves on the trip. There's nothing on telly and all the films are PG and not worth seeing.

After school, didn't particularly want to go home as Susie had gone to stay with Kate again, and Mum and Dad were going to be away till late on Dad's department's outing. Hope it will make them be nicer to one another, as they've been having more of their so-called 'discussions' recently. I was unwillingly drifting home, with nothing much to do, when I saw what appeared to be smoke signals going up from the Rec. I couldn't read the signals so went to investigate (this was me in my private detective role). It turned out to be some of my classmates trying to kill themselves with fags. Before I could open my mouth, they shouted, 'Here comes "know all" Pete' and '"I know what's good for you" Pete' and ' "You're killing yourselves" Pete'. They cornered me, puffing smoke in my face and chanting:

'It doesn't only damage your own health, but the health of those around you.'

'It kills about 100,000 people a year.'

'Each cigarette knocks five minutes off your life.'

'Every 15 minutes in Britain, someone dies of lung cancer.'

'It's lung cancer AND bronchitis AND heart disease.'

'It damages the baby inside the womb.'

'It's just like kissing an ashtray.'

'A quarter of all smokers get bumped off by the habit.'

I couldn't see why, if they knew all this, they still smoked, but they were perfectly happy to yabber on about WHY.

Ann said that she started when she was thirteen. Her older sister was going out with a heavy smoker. One night her boyfriend visited their house when their parents were out and he and her sister went to the back door (their mum wouldn't allow the smell inside the house) and began to smoke. The telly programme had finished so she went outside too. Her sister had said jokingly, 'Would you like a cigarette?' and she'd said OK, because she didn't want to look stupid in front of the boyfriend. Smoking was very strange and made her feel dizzy and hurt the back of her throat, but she carried on to impress her sister and the boyfriend. Now she got her fags from the corner shop, or bummed them off her friends.

Dave said that he got his fags from lots of different shops and though he was only fourteen, he never had any trouble buying them. He enjoyed smoking and thought it made him look big and hard, and said that if someone wanted to smoke it was up to them and nothing to do with anyone else. He started smoking when he and his cousin bought some cigarettes and tried them down by the river. He didn't like them much and at first only smoked at parties and discos. Later he had a lot of arguments with his mother and used to get very upset, but found that a fag 'sort of helped'. He hated girls smoking, as he thought it made them look common . . .

Ann butted in here and said she didn't see why girls smoking was any different from boys. She thought it made her look big and hard too, and sexy as well. She didn't think there was any point in her giving up, as her mum and dad smoked and her health was still in danger because she was breathing in their smoke anyway. She didn't seem to care what happened in twenty years' time, as we'd probably all be dead from the bomb . . .

[Another] kid wished he didn't smoke because it was crippling him financially – but he couldn't stop, especially as all his friends did it.

At the end they insisted on me having one, so that I knew what I was missing. They suggested that there was something wrong with me if I didn't smoke – or was it that I was too soft to try? Although I actually thought it would be bigger and harder of me not to try, I didn't risk saying so and had a drag, which didn't feel too bad, though it made me want to cough. In my role as detective, took two or three more really deep ones – and the top of my head began to fall off. I started coughing and getting pins and needles feelings in my hands. My eyes watered and I nearly fainted away. When I began to look as if I was about to throw up, my classmates, who had been killing themselves laughing, edged away.

. . . I stopped at the local shop to buy five packets of polos and chewing gum to cover up the smell. All I could see were packets and packets of cigarettes and endless adverts. Staring me in the face across the road when I came out, was a huge picture of a Formula 1 racing car advertising John Player Specials. Someone should get shot for that. In TINY writing at the bottom it said: DANGER: GOVERNMENT HEALTH WARNING: CIGARETTES CAN SERI-OUSLY DAMAGE YOUR HEALTH. What a lot of turds. Why let them have the advert in the first place, if smoking damages you? Got home, cleaned my teeth, ate another packet of polos, and held my breath when Mum kissed me goodnight.

Wednesday 25th December

Tore the last two pages out and started again. It's evening on Christmas Day. What I'd written before was too confused (like me), so I'm starting again, to try and sort things out. I'm struggling with so many different feelings and emotions, I can't cope. It's to do with Cilla, and me, and parties, and what to do next, or whether to do anything, all mixed up with me supposed to be feeling good because it's Christmas. That's in fact what started the whole problem off.

The reason I hadn't wanted to go to the party with Cilla was because the last party I had been to, with her there, was pretty boring. This was partly because everybody was drinking and I wasn't, partly because some gatecrashers came and ruined it, and partly because everyone else had a girlfriend. But this time Cilla was asking me. Mum said that I ought to go as I couldn't be unsociable all my life.

It was the first time I had been to a party knowing only one person. Till now, I've only been to parties with lots of people the same age as me, like all my friends at school, so on the whole they've been friendly and unthreatening. This one was different. Cilla's cousin is eighteen, so at fifteen, Cilla and I were the young-est by far, and personally I felt that I was totally different from everyone else and didn't fit in. But Cilla seemed to know every-body, and immediately went off leaving me in total isolation.

The party was in this huge drawing room, and I had to walk across it to a table, around which most of these strangers were sitting. At first I felt very self-conscious because I thought they were all staring at me, but I soon realised they were in fact totally ignoring me. I began to panic inside, when to my relief Cilla suddenly appeared and offered me a drink. I just took what she offered me and drank it down, almost without noticing what it was, I was so nervous and so anxious to seem hard. No one spoke to me, and I couldn't think of anything to say to them. Someone filled up my glass from a bottle on the table, and to cover my embarrassment, and give me something to do, I kept taking nervous sips of wine.

Then someone offered me some Pimm's No. 1, which I'd never had before. I gulped that down too. After a while, the combination of the wine and the music made me feel a bit more relaxed, and I started talking to someone who knew some people I knew. It was only when I got up to go and pee, that I realised how drunk I was. I knew that I shouldn't drink any more even if it did relax me and make me able to talk. Suddenly I seemed to lose my shyness entirely and I began to laugh hysterically at something someone said. Cilla came over looking very annoyed and tried to shut me up, but I just made things worse by talking a whole lot of rubbish to her.

As I talked I began to collapse and feel incredibly ill, I sat down, and then almost lay down, with my head between my knees, feeling all cold, sweaty and horrible. I thought I must be dying, I felt so ill. I was convinced Cilla would disappear in embarrassment, but actually she was very nice, and said that she'd ring my Dad, and come back with me. I threw up in the car on the way home. Luckily Cilla was sitting in the front. Mum made me drink lots of water, muttering something about 'preventing dehydration', and put me to bed. She was obviously absolutely spare, but didn't say anything. I don't remember too much after that.

On Christmas Eve I stayed in bed till lunchtime. I didn't feel like eating anyway. I had a splitting headache, and my mouth felt as if someone had made a compost tip in it. My first hangover. I could have done without Susie smirking and teasing me about getting drunk and liking Cilla. I doubted whether Cilla liked me. Even I didn't like me after last night. I remembered what a fool I'd made of myself, and wondered if it was going to ruin Christmas. Mum and Dad haven't said much about it, there's just an uncomfortable feeling around the house. Wish they'd say SOMETHING. I hung up my stocking, and heard Dad come in at 2 a.m., stumbling around and leaving a whisky smell behind him.

Today Susie and Sally came in to open their stockings with me. You'd think Sally was past stockings, but I think she wants to believe in Father Christmas even more than we do. Mum cooked a wonderful lunch. Noticed Susie had forgotten about being a vegetarian. Turkeys must count as chickens.

Subtle Dad gave Susie a drop of wine but not me. He said I'd had enough for the time being. I think I must have gone red, because Susie gave me one of her smug smiles. It provoked Sally though (who last year had done a special topic on alcohol) into announcing that nine out of ten children had tasted an alcoholic drink by the age of fourteen, and that most of these had tried it at home, closely controlled by their parents. At this, Susie took a 'closely controlled' gulp, spat it out, and said it was disgusting and she couldn't understand how people drank wine. I wondered how much of Sally's topic was done from personal experience! All this talk of alcohol made me feel sick again, so Sally stopped. She said she'd lend me what she'd written, if I was interested.

Brilliant presents from Mum and Dad – a new Walkman and some tapes. Sally gave me soap, Susie a handkerchief, and the much-needed electric razor came from terrible Uncle Bob.

Thursday 26th December
Boxing Day. Everyone else seems silent and a bit hungover. No sympathy from me. Played my new tapes. Bored by evening. Read Sally's 'Topic on Alcohol' so I could explain the dangers to my family.

Topic on alcohol by Sally Payne
Form VI Lower

Introduction
Alcohol is a chemical whose formula is C_2H_5OH. It is both a poison and a drug and was around long before Christ was born.

Wonder if Jesus ever got drunk? He seemed to do a lot of turning water into wine.

It's made by fermentation and can be produced from all kinds of things like potatoes, flowers, berries, etc., but the common alcoholic drinks are wine which is made from grapes, cider from apples, beer from hops and barley, gin from barley, malt or rye, flavoured with juniper berries. Rice makes sake, which is Japan's national drink.

A liquid containing just less than 50 per cent of alcohol by weight is called 'proof spirit'. This is because it contains the smallest amount of alcohol which, when gunpowder is soaked in it, would burn. At least 1,000,000,000 gallons of proof spirit are produced each year and mostly used for drinking. A small amount of alcohol will make people more lively, but larger amounts dull their senses and their brains and they may become unconscious or even die if they take too much.

Perhaps I could make a fortune distilling but I'd certainly remain a teetotaller myself.

Pure alcohol is called 'absolute' alcohol and is very difficult to make. The spirit used in industry and for cleaning paint brushes and things in the home is a mixture of ethyl and methyl alcohol. It is extremely dangerous to drink because the methyl alcohol is so poisonous. Sometimes people have added this to drinks as a joke and other people have been poisoned, blinded and have even died.

Felt as it someone did that to my drinks at the party before Christmas.

Facts about Alcholic Drinks
It's how much pure alcohol there is in a drink that is important, but additives which give drinks their colour, flavour, smell and taste also affect how bad the hangover is.

Half a pint of beer or lager = one measure (140 millilitres) of spirits (whisky, gin, vodka, etc.) = a glass of wine = a small glass of sherry = a bit less than half a pint of cider.

Hadn't realised that cider's even stronger than beer. Must be careful how much I drink. I always thought it was weaker, and just tossed it back.

Alcohol is rapidly absorbed from the stomach into the blood stream; most is burnt up in the liver and the rest is got rid of in sweat and urine. It is more rapidly absorbed on an empty stomach than a full one, and therefore it's better to eat before you drink. In general it takes the body one hour to get rid of one standard drink. More than five drinks at a party and you won't feel all right again till next morning. Drinking two and a half pints of beer or cider, or the equivalent, in an hour puts you over the legal limit for driving.

The Dangers
In the short term, the main danger is that alcohol affects your judgement, self-control and skills. Road accidents after drinking are the commonest cause of death in young men, and one in three drivers killed in road accidents have blood alcohols over the legal limit. The number of innocent people killed each year by drivers with blood alcohol over the legal limit is 12,000. Even AT the legal limit, you are four times more likely to crash.

I hope Sal's shown this to Steve, seeing how he rides his motorcycle.

The long-term effects of alcohol are, among other things: bleeding and ulcers in the stomach, cancer of the mouth and throat, brain damage, interference with your sex life, depression, psychiatric disorders, violence.

Wish Cilla would interfere with my sex life.

Drinking in pregnancy can also cause damage to the unborn child and it may be born very small, wizened, and brain damaged.
Women's bodies are more affected by alcohol than men's and therefore it does more damage to them.

I wonder if this is because men have more water in their bodies and therefore the drink would be more diluted than in women's?

Drinking in children – some of the facts that I could find:
- nine out of ten children try alcohol by the age of fourteen and this is the same for boys and girls.
- most of these try it at home.
- children who smoke also try alcohol.
- boys tend to drink beer and lager while girls prefer Martini and Advocat.
- children who are keen on drinking alcohol are more influenced by their friends than by their parents.
- boys and girls who drink a lot are seen by their friends as liking discos, going out a lot with friends, acting big and showing off, getting into trouble or fighting.
- boys and girls who never drink are seen as the opposite. – children who drink a lot are seen as being more disliked by grown-ups than by other children, and those that don't drink at all are the opposite . . .

Can see why she got an 'A' for this. It went on for pages and pages, but I'd had enough.

Saturday 28th December
Today was OK. It snowed, I really like Cilla. Especially after she was so nice when I was drunk. Hope she turns up at Sam's New Year's Eve party. Randy Jo's away, so I might get another chance.

Monday 30th December
Holidays are great because of sleeping in. Sam's mum rang to talk to my mum about their party. She thinks everyone will arrive with bottles of booze, and Sam's dad says he's going to frisk everyone as they come in. Poor Sam. Dad and Mum asked us what we thought about it at supper, but ended up as usual by telling us what THEY thought.

I said I didn't think it was right to go down the pub every night like Nick's dad who has a huge beer belly, and I wouldn't want to turn out like the tramps who hang out down at the shopping centre, clutching bottles of cider. I said I supposed it was all right to have the odd drink now and then.

Sally said that she had had her first drink when she was ten. Mum had given her a little white wine and she had pinched the bottle and finished it in her bedroom. There wasn't all that much left. After gulping it down she had felt giddy and heavy headed, and had had to lie down. She had taken it because she had always been so good and she wanted to do something against the grain. This really shocked Mum, who had had no idea that this had been going on, but both Mum and Dad had to admit that they got a 'bit merry' sometimes. (I didn't tell them that I had seen Father Christmas a bit more than 'merry'.) Sal said when she'd been out of work after failing her exams she'd felt really depressed and had gone down to the pub a lot, even though she didn't have much money. Now that she was working at the local hairdressers, and had decided to retake some of her exams, she wasn't drinking nearly so much.

Wednesday 1st January

NEW YEAR'S DAY – FEEL TERRIFIC! Went to Sam's party with Nick. Turned out we were both dreading it. Nick told me that there are three kinds of parties: brothel ones, at which the same music goes on and on as everyone is so busy, no one wants to get up to change it; booze-ups, at which everyone drinks lager or beer, it's mates only, and they all end up in the street, for fags and fresh air, or in the toilet, throwing up. Worst of all is the school disco, with teachers making fools of themselves trying to dance and wearing 'trendy' clothes. No touching drink or each other at these!

Nick said he was only going to have one drink this time. He'd got smashed at the last party so as not to feel left out, and had found his mouth telling people exactly what he thought of them. He had done the worst thing possible, drunk cider, then wine, then vodka, then beer. Even I could tell him to at least stick to drinking ONE kind of alcohol. He ended up lying down in the road with his mate, to see who died first.

Sam's party was great. Terrific music, lots of food and, like Nick, I stuck to one drink and saw the New Year in KISSING CILLA. After midnight things with Cilla got even BETTER. Hope this is a catching disease. It makes me feel really GOOD.

French Letters

■ *by 'Maxine Harrison'* ■

Maxine Harrison is a character created by Eileen Fairweather. Teen-ager Maxine has problems: she is fat, broke and her best friend, Jean has moved to live up North. She longs for glamour and romance in her life. It comes in the shape of her French penfriend, Jean who comes to London to visit her, but this creates its own problems. All of this is revealed in her letters to her best friend.

The extracts that follow are taken from:
French Letters: The Life and Loves of Miss Maxine Harrison, Form 4a, Eileen Fairweather (The Women's Press Limited, 1987)

Miss Jean Oglethorpe	*Miss Maxine Harrison*
The Queen's Arms	*96 Sheraton Road*
Furnace Street	*Hornsey*
Ashton-under-Lyne	*London N8*
Lancashire	*The South of England*
The Far North	*August 20th*

Dear Jean,

This morning my eyes were so puffy from crying I looked like Kermit the Frog with a hangover. Since you deserted London to live in the middle of nowhere I've cried non stop. Mum says I'll soon find another best friend, but that just goes to show she's got no heart.

As for your parents, someone ought to report them to the Child Cruelty people. Fancy dragging you away from all your friends (i.e. me) just so they can run a rotten old pub in the rotten old North of England. What was wrong with the Hornsey Tavern? It's no excuse, your mum wanting to live closer to your ageing nan. Fifty-six isn't that ancient, Joan Collins is fifty-four and she's in *Dynasty*. It'll serve your parents right if you do run away.

Yes, I did ask my mum if she'd adopt you, but she says the law wouldn't allow it seeing as you're already fourteen and you belong to someone else. Trust her to take the easy way out.

Still – about our bet. Have you had time to size up the local talent yet, or have you been too busy since yesterday unpacking? I've got to admit I've been getting cold feet – about whether our bet's *moral* or not, I mean. I'll write more about that tomorrow. Right now I've got to get on with crying. I miss you terribly.

Yours faithfully,

Maxine Harrison (Miss)

Dear Jean,

It's like this. I've been worrying all night about our bet and no offence but it *isn't* moral. When it comes to being the first to get a real boyfriend, you've got a head start. You live above a pub *and* you have a brother AND you'll soon be going to a mixed school. All I've got is a sister, a school that might as well be a convent, and a dad in a useless job. Well he might enjoy helping old ladies with their shopping trolleys, but what chance have I got of meeting anyone rich and famous on a bus?

What I'm getting at is that I don't think it should be like you said, with a flat prize of a fiver no matter *who* wins. Seeing as I've got all these handicaps and you've got all these advantages, I think we should have different odds on winning, like dogs do. So – if you're the first you should win at two-to-one, i.e. get two quid from me. But if I'm the first I should come in at five-to-one, i.e. get five quid off you.

I was going to increase the odds in my favour even more, seeing as I'm fatter than you. But then being the kind person I am I thought it wouldn't be nice to bankrupt a friend. Fat chance I've got of that, being ten stone four.

I hope you think this arrangement is fair. I think it is.

Today I miss you more than ever.

luv,

Max

PS In case your Maths is as bad as ever, this assumes our stake's a quid.

96 Sheraton Road, Sept. 10th

Dear Jean,

Well, the first day of term was typical. My sweet big sister Sue got the day off to a good start by kicking my leg in for borrowing her skirt. Then Bat-Face shouted at me cos I was limping so much I was late. Then Muck-Mouth Michelle made everyone laugh by saying probably I was late cos I'd come on my . . . dad's bus. Huh – so what if the number 14's never on time? I'm *proud* my dad makes time for all the old people to get on. If Michelle's dad was on the buses, he'd probably leave them to get run over.

Otherwise, the day was quite unremarkable.

You should see my leg where Sue kicked it – it's not just bruised its *dented*. She pretends to be so sophisticated because she's seventeen and works in a boutique, but really she's a yobbo. She's just jealous because it's me that's the brains of the family. Still, I suppose it could be worse, I suppose I could have a brother like you. But don't you listen to Bob – you've got a lovely nose. At least Bob the Dog lets you hang around the football club and get an eyeful of his mates. That one with the short shorts (?!) *does* sound a bit of all right! . . .

Anyway, enough from me, it's time to get my beauty sleep (har har).

luv

Max

PS I told a lie, there was one good thing happened at school today. In French, Hairy Henri asked who wanted a penfriend in France, and gave us a list of names to choose from. No one else was bothered, but I found a Jean on the list so have written to her. I like Jeans they are much nicer types than Michelles.

Londres, Oct 1st

Dearest Jean,

A pinch and a punch for the first of the month but only little ones seeing as I'm so happy – guess what, today I got MY VERY FIRST FRENCH LETTER! And French Jean isn't a girl SHE'S A BOY!!!

It's like this. French Jean twigged I'd thought I was writing to a girl, because I'd asked him things you only ask another girl. Like, are you on a diet, and is your bust big too? God, I'd never have told him about my problems Up Top if I'd known he was a boy Jean not a girl one.

Anyway, he was dead nice about it all and said I shouldn't worry about having big boobs because he REALLY LIKES BOSOMY GIRLS!!! I nearly died when I read that – I mean, it was dead embarrassing, but sort of made me want to faint, too. Anyway, he's seventeen, and dead good looking, and clever AND rich! He's very modest, though. He said it's just good luck he was born with so many advantages. You can imagine how long it took me to translate that mouthful! I think the only thing Jean isn't good at is languages. He wrote to me in French.

You'll never guess what his dad does – he's A BUSINESSMAN! Of course I didn't want to put him off, so I told him that my dad's the Head of London Transport. Well, that isn't a total lie – Dad *is* the Chief Shop Steward at his garage . . .

Gotta go – time for bed and (I hope) SWEET DREAMS! Do you think an English person can dream in French?

LOTSA luv,

Maxine

PS Saw Keith Edwards on the bus again, and he made a V-sign at Muck-Mouth Michelle instead of me. What did I ever see in that nerd? English boys are dead boring, that's what I always say.

A corner of the 'playground' (huh!)
Lunch hour
Oct 5th

Dearest Jean,

. . . I might as well admit it, I'm sick to my stomach and that's not just the school dinners. The way I see it, you're bound to forget me now that you've got that Sharon AND your dog AND that fella with the short shorts. I am jealous.

I'm only writing this letter to you now because it's better than standing in the playground on my own. I can't tell you how lonely I am. And it's so HUMILIATING. Every time the bell rings and we change classrooms I want to die, because I don't know if anyone will want to sit next to me. Mostly I end up lumped with the other rejects in the class, e.g. with Rosie S., that everyone now calls Slag-Bag because she's supposed to have DONE it. Michelle and Suzanne say that once you've done it people can tell, it shows in your face. I've looked and looked at Rosie but I can't see any difference.

I can't believe that only three months ago you were by my side, laughing at Bat-Face. Well, today she got her own back. She'd made us write one of those boring essays: 'What I Did In My Summer Holidays'. This morning she finally got round to handing them back, and in front of everyone she had a real go at me . . .

Smarmy nosey git, with her Greek tan. What *did* she expect me to write about – 'My Seven Boring Bloody Weeks in Boring Bloody Hornsey'? All she really wants to know is how much money we've got. Sometimes I wish to god I wasn't brainy. Then I wouldn't be stuck in the top stream with all the Suntan Snobs. Being brainy I don't fit in at home either. Mum's OK, but Dad's always saying the sooner I leave school the better. He reckons I should learn about the Real World.

Sometimes Dad gets all soppy and says he's only against me getting educated because of Today's Economic Situation. He's scared that I'll end up with some daft phoney government job like throwing beer cans down a sewer so I can fish them out

100

again. That's when he says that studying like mad'll only break my heart. Other times, Dad just says he's anti books because it's sitting around reading them that makes me fat. Sue says the same.

Well. I'd better end this letter before I make you want to end yourself. If you can think of ANYTHING to cheer me up, please write a.s.a.p.

I miss you. Terribly.

love,

Max

PS I forgot to say Ta for ringing. I LOVE your new accent. You're beginning to sound just like someone out of *Coronation Street*.

Hornsey N8, Oct 10th

Dear Jean,

Whoever said, 'A Friend In Need Is A Friend Indeed' must have been thinking of you. I was so touched by your letter that I even showed it to Mum. She was very impressed. She said that you sounded quite mature considering that you've always been such a bad influence on me. Anyway – I've been thinking about all your good advice, and you're quite right. It IS silly to think you can have only one friend in the world . . .

Luv yer,

Maxie

PS What do you mean, you want to know more about 'that girl Imelda'? There's nothing to tell. Her name's Imelda Maloney. She lives up the road, her parents are Irish, she's got about a million brothers and sisters, and she fancies Bob Geldof. I hardly know her really.

c/o 1 Sheraton Avenue
(posh, eh?!)
London N8
Dec 9th, 10 pm

Dear J,

I had to write and tell you straight away. Baby-sitting is AWFUL! I thought the kids would go straight to bed and I'd be able to watch the telly in peace, but I've only just got the little sods upstairs. And there isn't even a telly here! Can you believe it??!! Amanda and Nathan (that's their parents) reckon that telly warps people's minds. And tonight it's *Dallas*!

The kids are dead stuck up, too. They told me off for calling them Seb ad Al instead of posey old Sebastian and Alexandra. They didn't care WHAT I called them when I was teaching them what a firework was. But tonight they even told me off for calling them 'kids'. They said that's Degrading To Children. They should try Little Sods for size. They're only six and seven but they talk dead posh too, just like their parents. Amanda told me that *I* sound like someone out of *Eastenders*. I've been thinking about that. How come she knows about *Eastenders*, when they haven't got a telly?

Their flat's gorgeous though, it's just like Alexis's in *Dynasty* but a bit smaller. There's hanging plants hanging everywhere, and white sofas with no tea stains on them. You wouldn't believe it's just round the corner from Sheraton Road.

Gotta run, that's Blake and Krystle at the door.

luv,

Max

PS I found out how Amanda knows about *Eastenders*. Turns out she's a lecturer in Cultural and Communication Studies, whatever that is. Anyway, she says she can't criticise things unless she watches them first. So she watches videos of all the telly progs up at her college. What a hypocrite!!!

I wouldn't mind a job like that. Fancy getting paid to watch *Dallas*. I didn't watch *Dallas* OR get paid.

London N8, Jan 25th

Dear Jean,

I'm glad my letter inspired you re the usefulness of learning French. Your letter inspired me to try harder at Physics. You're right, there is something dead sexy about leaning over a bunsen burner with a boy. I can just imagine you and that Pete experimenting together!!??!!

. . . Mum and me *are* talking again. I'm so relieved. I hated hating her. We had a really good talk the other night, we stayed up till TWELVE. Mum said she didn't like having to be suspicious about Jean and me, but it would break her heart if I made the same mistake she did.

I do feel sorry for her. She says Dad's all right really, but that she's totally missed her chances. She wanted to be a top secretary but then she had to leave school at sixteen. Dad was the first boy she ever went out with. I reckon it's because Mum's a frustrated brainbox that she writes all those letters to people about the state of the world. She says she's brainy really, but working in a chip shop nobody believes that – not even me and Sue.

I felt dead guilty then so I said maybe she could go to college. She is thirty-five but they do take quite old people nowadays. Mum says she'd love to go but we need her wages too much for that. Anyway, she says life's ground all the confidence out of her. It was so sad we both cried and she became really sentimental. She said she was proud of me, that I'm the spitting image of her at fourteen, brains and all. She cuddled me and said that even when I'm a grown woman I'll always be her sweet baby and that I'm never to throw myself away.

I do love Mum, even if I am a battered child. She said she was sorry for hitting me and she never usually says sorry for anything. She even said she'd give me extra pocket money during the week Jean's here. She said she wouldn't do it usually but you're only young once and it is a *special occasion* after all.

I still think Mum's wrong though, about not letting Jean stay with us but I do understand her a bit better now. I feel very mature, generally. I look at the other girls in 4A who are still into Duran Duran and praise God for my tragic life. I know it's only because I've been forced to be older than my years that I'm not still a silly teeny-bopper too.

Me and Imelda start our new jobs tomorrow . . .

Yours in Maturity

Maxine

96 *Sheraton Road*
Hornsey
London N8
Feb 3rd

Dear Jean,

Guess what? I'm going to Paris instead of Jean coming here! Mum says that if I can save half the fare by Easter, she'll chip in the other half. She's opened a Post Office savings account for me, so that I can learn to budget, and every week she's going to bank her tips. People don't tip much in the sit-down part of a chippie, but she reckons that if she gives people bigger helpings on the sly, she should make enough to see me right. She said even Mrs Thatcher would steal the odd chip or two if it would help her children.

Mum's faith in the upper classes is amazing. She even said, seeing as Jean's dad is a businessman, she's sure she can trust his parents to see there's no hanky panky between Jean and me. Now all I have to do is wait for Jean's reply, telling me when I should

arrive. I'm sure he won't mind the change in plans. I've told him
that the mosquitoes in Hornsey are very bad at that time of year.
Paris in the springtime, here I come!

buckets of love,

Max

The Factory Annexe
c/o 1 Sheraton Avenue
London N8
Feb 9th

Dear Jean,

GREAT NEWS! Being a factory worker has paid off in more
ways than one – Amanda is now paying me better wages too! She
asked me to baby-sit tonight but I was VERY sniffy and said no,
thank you, I've got a better paying job. She asked me how much
I was getting and so now she's paying me £1.50 as well.

Actually she's paying me more than she knows cos I sneaked
the bottle tops over with me and got the Little Sods to stuff them.
They did at least half a gross between them and it totally knocked
them out – it's only eight-thirty and they're in bed already. I
didn't even have to read them Peter Rabbit.

I wonder what Jean would make of me being a Working
Woman. He's dead romantic. He says that his wife shouldn't have
to go out to work, she should have an easy life and only look
after him and his children and the home. Dead traditional. I told
Mum, and she sniggered that ALL wives are Working Wives it's
just that some don't get paid for it. God she's cynical.

I think Jean's got a point. If a man really loves you he doesn't
want you to stink of a chip shop like Mum. He wants the whole
world to know that *he* can take care of you. Mum says that even
if she does smell of chips at least she gets to see people. She says
that being at home on her own all day used to drive her batty.
She's got no romance in her. If I was at home all day I'd have
more time to think about my husband . . .

xxx

Max

Hornsey, Feb 13th

Dear Jean,

This morning I got Jean's reply and he's worried about a girl my
age travelling all the way to France alone. He's just like Dad. To
hear him, you'd think I shouldn't be allowed out of the house

except in a Securicor van. Jean says that anything could happen on a hovercraft. Like what? I've known about not taking sweeties from strangers since I could crawl . . .

Jean thinks he should be the one to put himself out. So he's suggesting we stick to the original plan – i.e. he'll come to stay in our Hornsey château. The worst thing is, Mum says I should be *grateful* Jean's so protective. I think it's just an excuse so he can have all the fun of travelling.

I love Jean from the bottom of my heart but I'd fight him on this one if I had a chance of winning. But I don't – Mum told me Dad hit the roof when she said she was sending me to France. The same old story – how I'd get robbed or murdered if I travelled more than five miles from home. If you ask me, Dad's in more danger of those things when he's collecting tickets on the number 14 bus. The truth is, he's MEAN.

Still, I'd rather be with Jean in London than not at all so I'll just have to bow down to fate, I suppose. I don't know how I'll break it to him that he's got to stay in a hotel. Mum says I should tell him NOW, because he'll need to book in advance. But I can't. Not yet. There's still a chance she might come round if I work on her . . .

The REALLY awful thing is that Jean hasn't even sent me a Valentine card. How am I going to face them in school tomorrow? Michelle's already got two.

Yours miserably,

Maxine

Londres, March 1st

Ma chère Jean (my dear Jean),

I've just had the most wonderful letter from France. Jean's excited about coming to London and finally meeting me that I've decided to stop feeling sick with nerves and get excited too.

We're going to have a GREAT time, I just know it. Jean wants to go everywhere. He's enclosed a long list – Madame Tussauds, The Tower of London, Buckingham Palace, the King's Road, Oxford Street, Regent's Street, Carnaby Street etcetera. The trouble is, I don't know where half those places are. And Mum never even lets me up Oxford Street on my own. She's got it into her head that drug pushers jump out of doorways and stick needles into your arm to get you hooked (HONESTLY!). She'd be better off worrying about the stuff that changes hands down at The Three Brewers. She'd never let me go to the toilet on my own if she knew what a den of vice Hornsey really is.

ANYWAY, the good thing about Jean wanting to do London

105

in style is that I've finally worked out how to sell the hotel idea to him. If he camped out here in Hornsey he'd spend half his holiday on the buses, trying to get to where the action is. So I've just written saying he'd be better off staying up town.

I'm a bit obsessed with money at the moment. The *bad* thing about Jean wanting to do the town is what it's going to cost. I've only earned twenty quid from the bottle tops so far and most of that went on that new dress. Do you think I should let Jean pay for me sometimes? Mum's always said that if you let a boy pay your way he'll expect to get *his* way in return. Other times she says that if a boy doesn't pay for you that proves he's trying to get you on the cheap. It's very confusing . . .

lotsa luv,

Max

PS I've been thinking. What if I don't like kissing??? I heard one of the girls at school say it's just like having a slug in your mouth.

Hornsey, March 15th

Dear Jean,

It's one a.m. and I'm writing this straight after THE PARTY. It was such a giggle I have to tell someone. Imelda would be shocked but I know you won't be.

Well, it seems Michelle didn't invite me because all of a sudden she LIKES me. Being such a brain-box I worked out that she just needed a load of girls to come cos she's got three brothers. All their mates were there, and she hadn't provided enough Talent. She also rounded up Rosie that she calls Slag-Bag, and Anna and Grace that she's always calling darkies. She calls *me* Snot the Swot nowadays.

Well, after a while Michelle started in on Anna and Grace. You know, calling them names. Anna took her shoes off and was all for stabbing Michelle with her stiletto but Grace stopped her. She's a Baptist and told Anna she should turn the other cheek instead of cutting Michelle's. I thought that was a bit wet myself even if I am nearly a Catholic.

Then someone turned the lights off and everyone started snogging. I didn't want to, so I went upstairs for a look around. Guess what I found in Michelle's bedroom? Anna and Grace, tossing all of Michelle's clothes OUT OF THE WINDOW!!!

It was that ever-so-holy Grace's idea. It's dead rainy tonight and she reckons that by the time Michelle's scrubbed the mud out of her clothes she'll have learned to keep a good Christian tongue in her head. She and Anna were giggling so loudly I had to keep guard. It was great. There were bras and knickers and skirts and socks flying all over Hornsey.

Michelle will never know who did it. Everyone downstairs was out of their brains. You should have seen the place. There were people spewing up everywhere. I counted two broken chairs and one broken banister and I left before eleven.

Now I see why Mum says I can't have a party here without her being in the house. I'm not even sure why I go to parties. I always have to wear the same thing, that old 'new' dress. I get all excited thinking I'll meet someone special who hasn't seen me in it before, but I always end up in the kitchen talking with the other girls.

Sue says I'm daft talking to girls at parties but I think it's better than snogging with someone you don't really like. Sue says I would get off with someone I liked if I made more of an effort to hide my brains from boys, but I said you can't hang your brains up with your coat. I thought that was a real clever answer.

I did neck a bit with someone at the party, though. I thought he looked sensitive as well as good looking. But then he started to snog with someone else straight after so he can't be. I felt dead tacky. From now on I don't think I'll even *think* of kissing anyone until we've had a PROPER DATE and I'm sure he likes me and I like him. I'd also like to be sure he won't KISS AND TELL. Keith Edwards was going round telling all the boys who he'd 'Done It To' before he'd even taken his jacket off.

Mum said something really funny. I didn't tell her anything about the party when I came in, but she must have guessed because suddenly she gave me a cuddle and said 'Cheer up, love, you've got to kiss a lot of toads before you meet Prince Charming.' She is a sweet old thing sometimes . . .

Hope you had a great Saturday night too.

Luv,

Max

Hornsey, March 20th

Dearest Jean,

Now for the GOOD news! When Jean comes I'm not going to look like an Oxfam shop reject after all. Thank God for catalogues!

Mum's friend Linda was over last night and accidentally left hers here. This morning . . . Mum found me flicking through it. I wasn't really putting it on, honest. I was just going 'Ooh' and 'Aah' and 'Look at those lovely clothes!' and sniffing and crying a bit. Suddenly Mum said, 'For God's sake, get out of that school blazer, I'm sick of the sight of it', and got on the phone to Linda and told her sign me up for EIGHTY QUIDS' WORTH OF CLOTHES!!!! Great!

Mum says I've got to pay the first four weeks instalments myself, from my savings account, to show willing, but that somehow or other she'll find the rest. God I love her.

I'm too excited to write more. I've taken the catalogue to bed with me and now I'm trying to work out what to choose.

Much love,

Max

Next Day, (March 2lst)

Dear Jean,

I heard so many opinions about what to get from the catalogue, that I didn't know *what* to choose in the end.

Mum said I should get something classic but Sue said that meant boring. Sue said I should get something trendy but Mum said that meant rubbish. Imelda said get something romantic but Frankie said that meant sexless. Frankie said get something low-cut . . . Dad just said, 'Bugger it, look at the interest rates.'

Then Sue pointed out that if I didn't make my mind up pronto, Jean would arrive before the clothes do. They take four weeks to deliver and Jean's coming in four weeks one day and six hours (April 19th, 10.30 am).

I got in a real panic and now I've ended up making everyone happy except me. I ordered the navy blue cardi that Mum said wouldn't date, the orange lurex top that Frankie liked, the green and orange spotted trousers that Sue chose, and some white high heels with sparkly bows that Imelda said were dead feminine. Now I'm worried they won't all go together.

Amanda said I should have stuck to my own taste, but I've never had enough money to work out what that is.

Oh – and I got a black jacket of course, like everyone's wearing. I wanted a bag too but as I'd reached my limit I'll have to stick to shoving things in my pockets. You've got good taste, so I'd love to hear from you that I've made a good choice.

Thanks,

Max

Hornsey, March 27th

Dearest Jean,

You've got to reply straight away, this is serious. What if when

Jean comes I get CARRIED AWAY? I suppose it's possible. My self-control's so weak – look what I'm like with Smarties.

It's all Mum's fault for forcing Jean into a hotel. She's so conventional she probably thinks my virginity's safe, so long as I'm back under her roof by night. But I know for a fact that lots of people do it before their official bedtime. Claire Rayner's always telling bored married couples to nip home for a bit in their lunch hour. I could always tell Mum we'd spent the day in a museum and she'd be none the wiser. God I'm scared. What'll I do? . . .

PLEASE write to me *a.s.a.p.* telling me how to keep my Hormones under control. Please, I'm depending on you. Sue's useless. You're the only person I dare ask. I miss you.

love,

Maxine

PS I'm glad our bet was never about HOW FAR we go! Thanking you for accepting the new terms. Basing it on marriage makes it *much* purer.

96 Sheraton Road
London N8
April 2nd

Dear Jean,

Thanks very much for your advice on how not to get into trouble. The only trouble is, what if it doesn't work?

I've thought about your advice a lot. I've even thought about the dangers. I've thought about the rotten names. I've thought about the health risks. What I still don't understand is – what if you know all about the horrible things to do with sex and you STILL get turned on?

There must be some reason people do it despite the risks of unwanted babies, abortions, bad reputations, infections, Herpes, Venereal Disease and AIDS. I think it's probably because it can be a lot of FUN. And exciting.

No offence, but your advice wasn't that much different from Mum's. The one good thing you said was, 'If you're not sure, you're not ready'. That got to me. I'd just re-read all my old copies of *Sweet Sixteen* and their agony aunt said that too. She reckons that if it's not the right person, and at the right time in you life, you'll be so tense it won't be any fun. So what's the point?

I think she's probably telling the truth, because from her photo in the mag she looks like a right little raver herself. Dead glam.

I've cheered myself up now so I'll love you and leave you (hah hah).

xxxx

Max

Tuesday April 22nd, 9 pm

Dearest best-friend J,

I'm knackered. Jean must have gone into every shop in Oxford Street today. Still he was happy and that's what counts . . . He bought STACKS of clothes! Three jumpers, two pairs of trousers, five shirts AND a gift-pack of briefs (I didn't know where to put myself when he was buying those!).

Jean wanted me to have some new clothes too, in fact he insisted. He found some beautiful classy clothes that he said would look much better than mine. But I couldn't afford them, so all I bought was some blusher.

I got a bit confused, trying to help him work out the difference between English and Continental sizes. Jean wasn't very pleased either that I kept tripping over him. But with these heels I couldn't catch my balance, especially as I had to keep my left hand in my pocket all the time. So that the assistants wouldn't notice that I hadn't got my wedding ring on. I was pretending I was his wife, you see. One assistant was very sweet, she said she could tell from the tone of Jean's voice that we'd been married a long time.

God, my feet ache. Jean was very protective about them. He found some lovely shoes for me, that were comfortable *and* pretty. I got MY FIRST PRESENT FROM JEAN! I didn't have enough for the shoes so he bought me a box of plasters. Then he told me to go into the loo and to put them on, and sponge my tights. He said the blood from my blisters looked disgusting. He's so sensitive, he was really upset for me.

Got to go now and soak my feet before they fall off. I'll have to try Sue's tip and stretch them with potato slices*

lotsa luv,

Max

PS * My shoes, I mean, not my feet!

THE CAPITAL OF ENGLAND
Wednesday April 23rd

Dearest J,

Do you like this new stamp of Princess Di? Jean says if I didn't

110

eat so much I could be as thin as her. He says the French really admire her, as she's the only Brit with good taste. I think Fergie's very stylish too so I felt hurt on her behalf. Also the Queen's.

Jean didn't like the Changing of the Guard today, he'd been expecting tanks charging up and down the Mall . . .

Then it was Now or Never – we were due for tea in Hornsey. On the bus I tried to prepare Jean for what he would find . . . I was dead nervous. But Jean fell asleep while I was talking. He told me later that it was the sound of my voice that did it. I think I must have been talking too quietly. And, as I had hoped, Jean was much too sensitive to enquire about our family's change in circumstances.

Mum's grub was great. She'd gone all patriotic so tea was ever so English. We had cottage pie, chips and peas, Orangeade and then ice cream with Chocolate Flakes stuck in. Sue had got in paper serviettes, and kept slipping saucers under the cups when Mum forgot them, and we acted like we were this sophisticated all the time.

Dad had on his wedding suit and did his best, apart from asking Jean had the French got electric light yet. I pretended to translate that but didn't.

It was a bit difficult having to be the translator for everyone. I did what I could with Mum's and Sue's questions, but as Jean didn't have a lot to say for himself there wasn't much to translate back. So I made a lot up, all about how much he liked our house and food and them and me and London and our Queen. Sue asked how come it took me so long to say in English what Jean took so little time to say in French. I told her that the words in French are all very short.

After a while though I found it hard to keep inventing Jean's conversation, so I didn't really mind when Jean left after only an hour and a half. It had been a strain on everyone. Especially on me. The worst was when Mum gave Jean a souvenir London bus and Dad went into a mad mime. I know Dad didn't know that he's supposed to be the Head of London Transport, but he could have been more subtle. He made me, Mum, Sue and Jean all sit in chairs lined up one behind the other, while he dashed up and down pretending to ring the bell and dishing out tickets like he does when he's working.

I don't *think* Jean twigged. And when we said goodnight by the hedge he was very sweet, saying he would always be grateful to me and my family. I asked him why, and he said that now he knew it really was true about the English being eccentric . . . God forgive me for running him down, but if he has one fault it's that he's a bit tightfisted.

Jean didn't kiss me goodnight, but maybe he was put off by

111

knowing that Mum, Dad and Sue were looking through the nets. I could tell because they'd switched off the light inside so they could see into the dark better.

It was a very nice day. Apart from the no kissing, I mean.

luv an' hugs,

Maxine

On the Circle Line, Friday, April 25th, 6 pm

Dearest Jean,

I've been sitting on the Underground for the past hour, just going round and round. I'm dead worried. Jean is expected home for a farewell tea but wouldn't come.

He said he didn't want to spend his last night in London in Hornsey. I left him outside the amusement arcade in Leicester Square. Jean wanted me to stay, but I said we shouldn't both let Mum and Dad down. Anyway, I'm sick of him playing those machines when I haven't got the money to play them too.

As it was his last day, Jean chose a really posh restaurant in Covent Garden. I only had an omelette and cup of tea. It set me back £6 and I didn't even get chips. Only salad. I didn't enjoy the sodding omelette either, being so worried about the bill. God knows what I'll do for money now. The first instalment on my catalogue clothes is due tonight!

Jean had told me he had to be careful because he was saving up for a Porsche so I didn't mind about him never paying for me before . . . He isn't hard-up, he's just mean! I must need my head examining. He said he needed good clothes for his career but today he forked out £80 (EIGHTY!) for a hand-made jumper from a trendy stall. Even I know that when he's a lawyer he won't be able to stand in court wearing a jumper saying 'I luv Princess Diana'.

Covent Garden's posey, I hate it. I started to tell Jean about how it was years ago, when it was a real market, a fruit and veg one. Before I realised what I was doing, I was telling him about Grandad being a porter there and how, before he scarpered on the family, he used to carry Mum around in a basket on his head when she was little.

I've always loved that story. But as soon as I said it I knew I'd blown it about us being posh. I panicked, and thought about spinning him some yarn but then I thought – bugger it, why should I? I've worked out what's wrong with Jean – he's a snob.

Why should I lie just to get on the right side of a snob? Probably a snob doesn't have one. Whatever you say or do or have they'll

112

always find a new way of putting you down. Mum's right, she's always said that people should take you as you are.

Today I caught Jean sneering at something and suddenly I thought, 'Well, mate, you're dead good looking and all that, but I'm Maxine Harrison and you can like it or lump it. And if you don't like it, that's *your* loss.'

Then we walked past the London Transport museum in Covent Garden, and I thought that would be as good a place as any to tell him the truth about Dad's job. You see, I've also had it up to here with Jean being rude all week to other bus conductors. I'd been thinking about that time Dad helped a woman have her baby on his bus, and about the other time when he and his driver were dead brave and drove a busload of screaming yobbos straight to the cop shop. I'll bet no pen-pushing businessman like Jean's father ever risks his life on the job.

Well – I did *mean* to tell Jean all this, but I've got to admit I chickened out. I know Honesty's the Best Policy and all that, but when you've told as many lies as me it's hard to know how to start putting it right.

Well, not lies really, just fibs.

I suppose if I'm going to be more Mature in the future I'd better start by getting myself home. I just hope Mum and Dad aren't too hurt. Or Mad. Especially with me.

Yours, sadder but wiser,

Maxine

96 Sheraton Rd
Hornsey
London N8
Friday, 11.30 pm late, Second instalment

Dearest Jean,

I feel so full of love I HAVE to tell someone. It's Mum and Dad you see. They've really cut me up. No, they didn't give me a rocket when I got in, they were so dead nice it hurt. And Mum had gone to such a lot of trouble too – you should have seen the cake, she'd iced a British flag and a French flag on it, all sort of intertwined. She's usually too busy to bake, but Dad told me she'd done it at night after I'd gone to bed so that it would be a surprise.

Well, that really finished me off. I'd been spinning Mum and Dad a yarn about Jean getting sick from our foreign water, but when I saw that cake I just burst into tears and told them the truth. Well, sort of.

Dad started mouthing off about inconsiderate foreigners but Mum gave him an eyeful and he went all sensitive instead. I think they must have had one of their 'Little Talks' about me. Anyway, he took me into the back garden to take my mind off things and got me to help him with some weeding. 'Pass the trowel,' he'd say, and then mutter something about their being lots more fish in the sea or how I was almost as pretty as a flower.

He didn't really cheer me up, he's my dad so he's bound to think me pretty, but he meant well and that's what did me in. I felt such a traitor, not sticking up for him.

Ditto Mum. She'd even got another present for Jean, a tea tray with a picture of Andrew and Fergie on it. For his Mum and Dad. I gave them a box of *Ma Cherie* chocolates saying it was for them from Jean, from Paris. Actually I bought them from Mr. Habib. He let me have them on tick.

Then Linda came round for her catalogue money but I managed to fob her off at the door. I didn't really lie, I just said Mum was out and I couldn't talk right now because I was suffering from Emotional Exhaustion. That's what the papers always say is wrong with pop stars when they're having nervous breakdowns.

Even Sue was nice, and lent me her second best shoes, so my blisters don't get any worse.

Got to go now. Sorry this is another depressing letter. Anything I write ought to carry a Government Warning, 'Letter Reading is dangerous for your Mental Health'.

Got to go now,

Bye

M.

Second Cubicle
The Super Loo
The Station
JUST AFTER SEEING JEAN OFF
(April 26TH, 11 AM)

My dearest one and only Jean,

Please wash your hands after you have read this. I am writing it in a toilet. I just couldn't wait to tell you the goods news. Jean's gone and I DON'T GIVE A DAMN! REALLY!

Now my blisters can heal. I brought my flatties in a plastic bag to the station, and the minute I'd waved him off, I dashed in here to change. I nearly didn't wear the heels to the station, but I couldn't resist giving Jean one last peek at my legs. I want him to feel sick as a pig about what he'll be missing.

I don't want him to suffer too much, but I wouldn't mind if he is as sick as pig for a while. Give him his due, he did look a bit ashamed when I gave him a slice of the cake Mum had baked for him. I presented it on the Fergie and Andy tea tray, with a little servile curtsy. Then I said that if he didn't like Mum's gifts he was welcome to throw them under the wheels of the train. I said that we wouldn't mind because it was 'well-known that the working class don't have feelings'.

I said all this with a big smile, like it was a joke, but I wanted him to know that I'd twigged how snotty he is and that I'd never let him get away with it again. I know that there'll never be another opportunity but I don't care. I only cried for five minutes in the Super Bogs before I started to feel relieved, and five minutes is nothing.

I'm glad I was proud. Jean tried to give me a last kiss, but I pulled away. I said I was going down with Hay Fever, and didn't want to give him germs. Pulling away from those big manly shoulders was one of the hardest things I've ever had to do. He still looked gorgeous in his suit, even if it was more mustard than lemon coloured after a week in London. We both said we'd write, and we both knew we never will.

Even if he is a snob he'll always have a place in my heart. I don't think I'll ever be able to throw away Jean's photo.

My First Love – gone. Forever, Oh damn, now I've made myself cry again.

Don't worry about me, I'm not really heartbroken. But please write or ring AS SOON AS YOU GET THIS.

I miss you, my one and only Jean,

Maxie

Message from the Falklands

■ *by David Tinker* ■

David Tinker was born on 14th March 1957. In 1974, after a private school education, he went to Dartmouth on a scholarship to train as an officer in the Navy. He qualified in 1976 and finished his training aboard *HMS Fife*. In October 1976, the Navy sent him to Birmingham University to study History. There he met his future wife, Christine. They got married in the Spring of 1980 and bought a run-down cottage in Shropshire.

Meanwhile, David had been posted to *HMS Hermes*, the biggest ship in the Fleet. Early in 1981, to his parents' surprise, he transferred from the Seaman branch of the Navy to the Supply branch. This involved a period of retraining and reflected his growing disenchant-ment with the Navy and his dislike of being separated from his wife. His new appointment was as secretary to the captain of *HMS Glamorgan*, a sister-ship to *Fife*.

By this time, Christine had qualified as an officer in the Women's Royal Army Corps and she was posted to Chatham. David was keen to get a posting to a shore establishment too so that he could spend more time with her. This was the main reason he had given for wishing to transfer. In September 198l, he was told that his next posting would be to Chatham. In the meantime, *HMS Glamorgan* went about her duties. In March 1982, they set off for Gibraltar for a big NATO exercise, *Springtrain*. David assumed that this would be his last tour of duty on board ship.

The extracts that follow are taken from:

A Message from the Falklands: The Life and Gallant Death of David Tinker, Lieut. R.N. from his Letters and Poems, compiled by Hugh Tinker (Penguin, 1982)

To H and E *HMS Glamorgan, 2 April 1982*

[Hugh and Elizabeth – his parents]

Thank you for your long letter. This is just a quick one to say that today we have heard the news that we are off to the Falkland Islands to bash the Argentinians. This is great fun, and very much like Maggie Thatcher to stick up for our few remaining colonies with a show of force! A great Fleet is assembling, both our car-riers, *Hermes* and *Invincible*, the two County Class destroyers, *Antrim* and ourselves, three Type 42 destroyers, three Type 21 frigates (both classes are very modern) a nuclear submarine, *Superb* (sshh) and *Brilliant*, *Exeter*, and two store ships: with *Endurance*, sixteen ships down there.

At the moment we have just cancelled the exercise. We are transferring stores, and are just about to set off south from the Gibraltar exercise area. We are due to call in at Ascension Island and pass by St Helena: very much a 1914 affair, with the Royal

Navy going off to defend her colonies (or should I be thinking of Suez?). The Americans, this time, seem to be on our side, but we have only heard 'buzzes', not having had newspapers for some time. It is anyway all very exciting.

Unfortunately, it means I shall miss moving into our cosy married quarters for another couple of months, and Easter leave goes by the board. But this is much more fun. Surprisingly, the Argentinians have quite a good navy: a carrier with strike aircraft, (like the old *Ark Royal*) and three Type 42 destroyers. If *Superb* sinks the carrier we will take care of the rest.

Of course, the whole thing may blow over in a week, but the thrill of some real confrontation away from the nuclear bombs of the northern world in a 'colonial war' is quite exciting compared to the usual dull routine of exercises and paperwork (although these will still continue: we shall probably 'work up' as we go south).

. . . All for now, as this must be posted before the ships separate and we head south for the penguins.

To Christine   *HMS Glamorgan, 7 April 1982*

This is, in fact, the last letter that I will be sending you for a while until Chile starts sending our mail back for us. But then, of course, it will be censored and even though only by the padre, doctor or dentist [they are] not people who I want to read my personal thoughts to you. I love you very much indeed and hope that you are not worrying about it all. It is much easier for me, here, because it is really very exciting, but I know how I would feel if you were away. Rest assured, that even if the worst happens . . . I am in one of the best places in the ship. I shall be in the hangar or on the Flight Deck all the time. The hangar is the best protected place, with thick double doors, and the life rafts are right next to us. We have extra water and are stocking up with chocolate and biscuits which we'll carry in our gas mask bags. If it hasn't all been solved by the time we get down there we shall be sleeping on camp beds in the hangar where it is only a five seconds dash to the open. We wear very thick clothing all the time and have plastic suits which cover us completely (like a big bag) for jumping into the water. The life rafts are also very good with stocks of water, radios, etc. I am only telling you this so that you know we are in the best position possible to survive, on the Flight Deck. I am sure it won't come to it anyway. The Argentinians must be frightened so see such a large fleet coming towards them.

If it does come to a war there won't be much of a naval battle. Our submarines can take out their aircraft carrier and Type 42s [destroyers] (built in Barrow!) and we can take care of the rest.

All our weapons are designed for their generation of forces. I doubt if the Argentinians will want to risk sending their ships out. If they are sunk, they will have nothing to stop us bombarding Buenos Aires. — even said, 'Drop a big white job (Polaris) on them.' Thank goodness he's not in command.

The main threat is from air attack, and all our ships are air defence ships: with, of course, the Sea Harriers, which are very good. We have Seaslug and Seadart long-range anti-aircraft missiles, and Seacats and guns for close range. And we have got plenty of them!

The most amusing thing is that it will be difficult to find the Falkland islanders [amidst all the combatants]. With only 1,800 of them, there are, I suppose, 15,000 RN personnel, 4,000 army – 4,000 Argentinian army, and say 3,000 Argentinian navy: outnumbering the islanders by about twelve to one!

The good thing about it is that there is stacks of time left for some sort of compromise. Which I am sure will happen. Things seem to be happening slowly but surely on that front. More and more allies for us (including the French) a base in Chile, mediation by the USA etc. We get all our information from the World Service of the BBC (just like *Yes, Minister*) although our own signals tell us what our own forces are doing, which is circulated by 'buzz'. As you can imagine, the whole ship is throbbing with buzzes . . . All the talk is about the latest developments; how each person thinks we should fight the war; the ups and downs, as the situation unfolds; . . . The sailors are all very amusing with their jokes about it all.

The advent of this whole new lifestyle is really quite strange. Normal days and weeks are put into abeyance. Routine paperwork becomes unnecessary. The ship's programme becomes non-existent. We're here, until something else happens. There is no set pattern or framework for it all. The comforts of life, and the goodies – leave, pay, fun time in foreign ports – all become irrelevant. We are now actually doing something which we have always thought about as likely as Men on Mars!

To Christine   *HMS Glamorgan, 10 April 1982*

You may have been wondering whether or not to move into the Married Quarter, but I should think you have gone ahead anyway. My guess is that I won't be back for some time – probably September – and then, of course, appointments, turnovers etc. have to be re-arranged so it may be as late as October before I get to Chatham. It all depends on whether a settlement can be reached, but even then we may be left to patrol the area . . .

. . . As we get nearer we have lost the euphoria – accompanied by depression – and are getting more determined that we must do our job well to defeat the Argentinians and survive. Reality is dawning rapidly.

At times the situation seems so absolutely silly: here we are, in 1982, fighting a colonial war on the other side of the world: 28,000 men going to fight over a fairly dreadful piece of land inhabited by 1,800 people. After it is all over and millions of pounds have been expended they will be left in peace (having had their homes destroyed by shelling) and the 28,000 men will then go away again. Moreover, one side [Britain] has supplied the other with its weapons so that the war can be started in the first place – and both sides end up impoverished.

The *ideal* is most praiseworthy: the wishes of a tiny people being supported by the might of a large industrialised state. Everything else is quite ludicrous. It has given us some time in the sun, and a break from the horrid, rough weather up by the Shetlands – just in time for the horrid weather of the Falklands! It is interesting, anyway, preparing to go to war; even if, hopefully, everyone sees sense before long.

It is certainly something I have often thought about before now; and to a certain extent a boy's upbringing is centred on warlike activities and war stories. If we can have a few shots over the bow that will be quite enough, and honour will be satisfied. I personally do not want to kill any Argentinians, or anybody else . . .

It is a very unreal time. All the preparations for war are carried out, which one always thinks of as happening in war films only: but are actually happening now. It is almost like a gigantic spoof. Time is also unreal. The days pass at their usual speed, but it seems ages since we left Gibraltar – yet only two weeks ago. The longest time was when *Hermes* etc. were preparing to sail. It seemed weeks before they were ready, but in fact only a weekend: and amazing for Pompey dockyard! It must have been a fascinating sight to see all the preparations taking place, I wish I had been there. It must have been a bit like D-Day. We have also been hearing wonderful things about the speed of the dockyard since then also . . . The most odd thing is not having a ship's programme and not having a calendar of 'days left to go in *Glamorgan*', I am still holding the count-down at 15. The best thing, I suppose, for us both is to live day to day. Each day comes with its own small achievements and blessings, and there is contentment in living like that. Certainly there's no point in being depressed by looking at too big a chunk of the future.

To Christine *HMS Glamorgan, 12 April 1982*

It's been a bit of a working Easter, here. It must be the first time I haven't been to church on Easter Day . . .

The *Portsmouth News* was of course full of the send-off for *Hermes* and *Invincible*. Enormous photographs: flags waving, mothers weeping, etc. All good stuff. Now we have had the fun of it all, let's go home.

Things look much more hopeful for a successful conclusion by negotiations. The Argentinians have withdrawn their navy, sensibly; and the Falklanders must surely see that they won't get exactly what they want over this war. Either they have a huge battle and remain British for a few more years before the Argentinians try again when we haven't got a Navy left, or they accept a compromise. Once people in Britain see that inflation is going up because the pound is falling, and that they have to pay for a war or naval patrol in taxes, then they may get fed up with the Falklands anyway. Wars are always economic disaster for a country (apart from our 19th-century colonial wars) so let us finish it while we are still at the flag-waving stage and enjoying it all. Honour would be satisfied if one of our submarines could just sink a small Argentinian ship (preferably without loss of life).

To Christine *HMS Glamorgan, 16 April 1982*
At Ascension Island

The news of the war front is more and more exciting. The Argentinian Fleet putting to sea, so we might get a chance to sink them (although I doubt that they'll venture outside Argentinian coastal waters). Twenty RAF ground attack Harriers coming on the next container ship (as opposed to ours, which are interceptors). More troops coming in the *Uganda*. And tons of ships coming in a month's time, including *Illustrious* (our *third* aircraft carrier) which hasn't even done the Portland work-up yet. And the French are going to provide air-launched Exocet missiles (*the* missile we are scared of from the Argentinians: twenty miles range, sea-skimming, and almost invulnerable) for our helicopters to carry: in addition to 'Sea-Skuas' for our Lynx helicopters. This wasn't due to enter service until 1985, and is even better than Exocet. Ho ho ho: spend lots of government money, depress the pound, put up inflation: what fun! Man is the most extraordinary animal.

I cannot believe that the Argentinians will want to fight with all this lot coming against them. Already they look to be in danger of spending all their foreign currency reserves and losing all ability to obtain loans in the western world. Surely they must give in soon: hopefully, over the weekend, and then we can all go home.

I suppose you must be pretty fed up of hearing about the

Falklands, but it is quite exciting being at a particular spot where all the front pages of the newspapers are focussing on. Something that I will never experience again. I was looking at *Hermes* today, where the journalists are, thinking that in the British press just *here* is where the Number One story in the world is coming from. I'm sure you would feel just as excited about it all if you were here. It is also special because it is something that you can't just 'get in on the act' in, and something that we are all caught up in: and can't get out of. Something where you see the forces of Government and State dictating to the individual to do something he doesn't want to do at all. It's quite fascinating.

We are now fully prepared for 'war'. My cabin is secured for action. It looks very tidy. And we all have our dog tags – Geneva Convention ID Cards, and first field dressings. Giving them out yesterday was a sobering thought for most people; reminding them that the 'From the Cradle to the Grave' Service was now catering for situations where they could be blown to bits, interrogated, or laid out on a slab. Not the sort of things one wants to be reminded of! (And I wouldn't mention them in this letter if I thought that there was the remotest chance of any of them happening . . . I am *definitely* leaving the Navy in the next round of redundancies if I can. Doing warlike things is quite fun, but peacetime activities are dreadful.

Everything is now painted in wartime colours and looks very dashing. The helicopter is now dark blue, with black lettering and roundels of red and light blue. The Harriers are similarly dark grey. On the Flight Deck you can now do 'wartime' things. I landed a Sea King helicopter on deck the other day; once in daylight, and once at night. You are not supposed to, because they are much too big; but it was great fun and much more convenient for people getting in and out, than slowly winching them up. I want to land a Harrier on deck next! I am sure it would fit OK.

That's all from 'War Special' for the moment . . . I suppose you will stay in barracks for the moment, will you? You'd find it pretty horrid coming home to an empty quarter every night. I hope everything else is going OK . . . This news that *Glamorgan* is right at the back of it all should put your mind at rest and allow you to concentrate on the important things of life, like tennis . . . All my love comes to you with this letter . . .

To Christine *HMS Glamorgan, 17 April 1982: 10 p.m.*
At Ascension Island

This is it: the buzz has come that we are being ordered south, in command of a force of nine ships. *Hermes* and *Invincible* are remaining at Ascension to wait for their aviation fuel. The Captain/Commander won't tell us where we are going, or even that we are going, but will probably come up on the broadcast tomorrow, saying that we have been lucky enough to be selected to go south – and next mail will be in three months' time! I have dashed up to write this letter to you to let you know: a helicopter will take it ashore tomorrow morning, so it should get to you. It's very much 'Like wrongs hushed-up, they went'. In the middle of the night, without even being told we're going.

Let us hope that by the time you read this the Argies will have settled, or that we have gone to South Georgia – who knows? There are still 2,000 miles between us and them . . .

It is unfortunate that we are leaving the *Hermes* group as the press won't now be able to report back where *Glamorgan* is, so I doubt you'll see any mention of us. I don't even know where the other ships are which left previously. Let us just hope that everyone stays cool . . .

Anyway, lots of love for now. Next letter follows in two months' time: less, if the Argies and Maggie see sense.

To Christine
HMS Glamorgan, 3 May 1982
At the Falklands

Although the mail doesn't go off that often now I am hopeful that this will reach you before too long via one of our returning storeships. I am sorry that there's been a long gap in letters but . . . we are all fine out here. The weather is not as bad a they make out. Just like England in fact. Yesterday was a lovely sunny day with a very calm sea. The wildlife out here is super, and so much of it! Some beautiful albatrosses have been following the ship with their enormous wings . . . Also, some lovely white doves; brown, well-fed looking birds (a bit like our Penguin); geese with long necks and plump black and white bodies. They all fly round regularly when we are close to land. It's very nice looking at them all on the Flight Deck when we are at action stations (we thought we should take some bread up to feed them, as the war rages around). The Falklands themselves look a bit like the Shetlands: it all looks very peaceful and still, in there.

The war has gone fine so far. The stories from South Georgia are quite amusing. When the British troops (79) advanced into the main square they found the Argentinians sitting round the edge, smoking, weapons piled in the middle, already to give in against superior odds. The sea battles have produced some good results as well: one cruiser, one submarine, and two patrol craft lost by the Argentinians. The Harriers are proving very good indeed; stopping Argentine aircraft at seventy miles away.

The war for *Glamorgan* started on 1 May (a date I won't forget), as the main force moved towards the Falklands we went on ahead to do some shelling of the airport . . . The Royal Marines on the signal deck . . . strapped to the Oerlikon guns, very exposed, shouted to the Mirages as they went past, 'Come here you buggers, let me get at you.' The Argentinians claimed us as damaged, but this was only because we engaged our gas turbines with a will, and set up an enormous plume of smoke. They actually didn't touch us. The outcome of it all was that we are not going to do shelling again in daylight, but only at night, when their aeroplanes can't fly for various navigational reasons. It is quite safe then. They only have howitzers which can't shoot us moving around . . .

I hope things haven't been too bad for you at home. It must be most frustrating when you hear the news of all this instantly, but don't get a letter to say how we are for weeks. Anyway, no news is good news. It is amazing though how quickly these events are broadcast. We started our barrage at 7.15 p.m. and fell out from action stations at 9.30 p.m. By 10.00 p.m. it was in the BBC World Service news, having gone via Argentinian fighter pilots to Argentina, and then to the press, and then to London and the BBC. And we heard about the torpedoing of the Argentinian cruiser on the radio half an hour before the signal came from MOD confirming it . . .

Don't worry about us here. We are all in very good spirits, laughing and joking. The sailors' humour remains very funny in these circumstances. I often think of you, and think you would find a lot of their stories amusing . . .

To Julian Salmon   *HMS Glamorgan, 6 May 1982*

Thank you so much for writing, Julian, with your marvellous peaceful message. There is very little of that here, as you can imagine, and it is very welcome. We live on an air of tension here, not sleeping but just dozing, ready with our gear, waiting for the action stations buzzer announcing another air raid. The picture that Nott and his cronies are giving is not true. The Argentinian air force has the latest attack aircraft and missiles, which we just do not have. We long for nights, when their aircraft cannot attack us, and at the moment we are rejoicing in a fog which is sheltering us. I wish the politicians would see sense and stop the war. What is happening here is barbaric and totally unnecessary. It is disgusting that two Christian and humane countries (one at least!) should resort to this, all for some petty reason.

Do you remember when we were studying Wilfred Owen at Mill Hill? In this poem where he says, 'Oh death was never enemy of ours . . . We whistled while he shaved us with his scythe,' he ends up (I'm probably misquoting), 'There'll come a day when men make war on death for lives – not men for flags.' This is what it is, a war for a flag . . . I think that Maggie Thatcher sees herself as a Churchill, and as for Nott . . . let him come and lie down on the deck with us while the air raids come in and the missiles go off. He would see what it is really like and soon change his tune.

I never would have thought that I would be writing to you in the middle of a war! Let us hope that it ends SOON . . .

To H *HMS Glamorgan 22 May 1982*
[received 10th June]

I haven't mentioned much about the war and our part in it in my letters to Elisabeth and you, and to Christine, so as to try to avoid upsetting and worrying them in addition to the worry they must already feel, especially when the news is so regularly ghastly. However, I will to you, because you know what it's like; with six years' worth, it won't seem so unexpected. We still cannot believe we are at war, even while it's going on, and when I have had a good night's sleep I wake up without remembering the war for a while. Our surroundings, of course, are exactly as normal: and we are very used to doing perpetual exercises. We still have proper food, hot water to wash with, etc. There are a few differences; covers and fabrics have been thrown away, the scuttles (windows) permanently blacked out, the chests tied down, no loose papers about but life has its flashes of normality. I sometimes have some typing to do, we have 'Requestmen' and 'Defaulters', the NAAFI sells chocolate, and we still have 'Elevenses' (at Stand Easy). As we don't have personal weapons there's no particular feeling that we are fighting. We are mostly a peaceful bunch who would not want to shoot anyone. The war just happens; we do shelling of shore positions and we get attacked by aircraft. We dislike both, and the time when everyone is relaxed and happy is when we are 'legging it' away from the action at 29 knots. On one such dash, 120 miles after the raid on Pebble Island, where the SAS and our guns destroyed aircraft on the ground (14 May) we used 33,000 gallons of fuel – 6 yards per gallon! We can always rely on the engineers to get us out as fast as possible. Blow the expense on fuel!

The actual war part of it is not so much frightening but tense. In the first week when the fleet was closer inshore (70 miles) and continually under air threat some people were getting to their nerves' ends, especially those in the Operations Room where the war is fought from (all the radar screens, communications, and missile buttons are there, and they have to react quickly to air attack). However, after the *Sheffield* incident the Fleet moved further away out of range, and the alarms grew less . . .

After that it was bombarding Stanley, same place, same time, on the 16th, 19th and 20th May – *Glamorgan* only – we were a bit jumpy about going back there three nights in a row: surely they would get wise? But fortunately they did not react very much. On the BBC this was classed as a 'dangerous mission . . . in a possible minefield'. The Admiral said it would be a piece of cake. And no one told us about the minefield. We did see the Argentinians firing at each other. They were obviously jumpy. On the last night we lit ourselves up with flares: we all jumped for cover on the Flight Deck. Nobody had warned us this would happen as we were only a mile off the coast at the time, and similarly nobody told the engineers we were going to drop scare charges and they thought we were being torpedoed . . .

Anyway, we did a good job of scaring ourselves, if not the Argentinians, and the Admiral was pleased (and amazed?) that it had gone off safely. We had commenced these raids at a regulation 8 knots with super-duper modern anti-submarine countermeasures but by the end we used good old-fashioned zigzagging madly and steaming at 24 knots. We were mightily relieved when we legged it from our first '0230 to Port Stanley, calling at Stork Bay, Beacon Point and Beauchamp Channel'.

That night the landings went in and it is now the second day that they have been ashore. Fortunately, the poor ships still in there have not been attacked today and should come out tomorrow. It has been a dreadful price in ships to pay – one ship for every four aircraft. If we could fight them in the open sea our chances would be so much better. I would much prefer that their air force just did *not* fight but it looks like the only way to end this will be to break the back of their air force (we have destroyed about fifty out of two hundred). Despite what the press and public opinion say, they are brave men who have to do their duty as we do.

I suppose that this sort of naval war is quite different from your war when you had to put up with a lot more . . . These last three weeks have seemed long enough and we don't like to think any more into the future than the end of the day. We are lucky in that we can rescue our survivors and send them back to England, and our living conditions are fine; but air attack by these very fast jets coming in low is not very nice.

The pity for us is that there is no cause for this war; and, to be honest, the Argentinians are more patriotic about the Malvinas than we are about the Falklands. And the iniquitous thing is that we trained and equipped them! Their carrier, Type 42 destroyers, submarines and aircraft are all European. Britain even sold Argentina the maps of the Falklands a month before the invasion so that there were no maps for our own troops when we needed them. We were about to train their Lynx helicopter crews to use the Sea Skua missile (in May). That's the only advantage we have over their ships at present. And we even gave them an official cocktail party when one of their Type 42 destroyers was training in Portsmouth last year! . . .

Still, I suppose this is all an experience one should go through if only to drive home for each generation how stupid war is . . .

Certainly the trivia of life and the important things are all brought to mind by this. And how much the trivia are at the forefront of normal life and the important things put away, or not done, or left to do later and then forgotten. Here, certainly, the material things are unimportant and human 'things', values, and ways of life are thought about by everybody.

To Christine   *HMS Glamorgan, 23 May 1982*

How I love you: so very much. You are absolutely wonderful. You have been very brave indeed over the past weeks, and I am very proud of you. You seem to be standing up to it so very well: much better than the other wives and it really heartens me to know that you are not letting it get you down too much. Although I know and feel for you, that you have been going through agonies over the casualty and damage reports from the landings. It has been about three days since they first gave details of casualties, and even now they haven't said who, and which ships (I hope that's because they informed next of kin *first* this time and didn't just bleat it out over the news). It has been a horrible time for you, and I have been feeling for you all through it. We were 100 miles away from the landings with the carriers, and nothing came out to us . . .

. . . Just keep going from day to day as we all do, and eventually it will be over. I am very proud of you Christine. You are a girl in a million, and you're mine and I love you. Nothing is more important than our love which can't be hurt by anything. It has grown stronger and stronger over the past five years we've been together, and it will stand the test of anything. It is unassailable. It gives me total fulfilment and happiness in life which I never had before I met you, and I know it is the same for you. When we are together again I will be able to comfort you, console you, and love you. But even now that we are apart it's still there, with a confidence and a warm glow. It is complete, ultimate, and assured. It is a perfect and pure love that lasts for ever.

To Jonathan and Helena   *HMS Glamorgan, 28 May 1982*
[his brother and sister-in-law]   *[received 21 June]*

Thank you very much for writing. I received your letter via the 'reinforcements' which arrived a couple of days ago. It is very nice to know that you are thinking of us and I appreciate your thoughts.

Although you say it seems very unreal in England it's also very unreal here. Even when, on the first day, we had just been attacked by their Mirages we were saying to each other that it couldn't be real. Why were we fighting *Argentina*? And who wanted to live here [in the Falklands] anyway?

I cannot think of a single war in Britain's history which has been so pointless. They have always been either for trade, survival, maintaining the balance of power, world [economic?] growth, etc. This one is to recapture a place which we were going to leave undefended from April, and to deprive its residents of British citizenship in October. And to recapture it, having built up *their* forces with the most modern Western arms (not even *we* have the air-launched Exocet which is so deadly). And fighting ourselves without the two pre-requisites of naval warfare: air cover, and airborne early warning, which have been essential since World War II . . .

Not only has Mrs Thatcher survived a political fiasco; she has covered up the military cost to Britain (ten times what it will cost the Argentinians) and sent a fleet to do a job it should never have been sent to do: because of no air cover resulting in four ships sunk, four written off, and more damaged. She has become a complete dictator, ordering war without consulting Parliament, and she is dragging the masses, shouting and cheering, behind her. The newspapers just see it as a real-life 'War Mag', and even have drawings of battles, and made-up descriptions, entirely from their own imagination! If some of the horrible ways that people have died occurred in *their* offices maybe they would change their tone. Let us just hope it ends quickly.

If we do recapture the islands we will still have to talk to the Argentinians, and I doubt if Mrs Thatcher will compromise at all: in which case we will have to provide a garrison of about three Servicemen to every one inhabitant and spend millions of pounds on all the military installations that will be necessary and keep at least a submarine, two ships, a squadron of aircraft, AA missiles, a radar early warning system, anti-ship land-based missiles, and a garrison of soldiers there. They will need married quarters, sickbay, school, NAAFI, etc. The whole thing is totally ludicrous.

What Mrs Thatcher does not realise is that the Argentinians *believe* that the Malvinas are theirs. They have sent pilots on suicide missions against us, on a one-way journey, because we are out of their range: so they effectively double the range of their aircraft by not going back. And they don't have any sea-rescue helicopters to pick up the pilots afterwards. In fact, the bravery of all their pilots shows that they are more than 'mildly' interested in the Falklands.

The sad thing about all this, of course, is that the professional forces of both sides (not the conscripts) do what they are told. So if two megalomaniac idiots tell them to beat each other's brains out, they do; and there is no stopping them. Our own frigates were ordered into a similar suicidal position in Falkland Sound and stayed there until ordered out again, after 80 per cent were sunk or badly damaged. I am sure the troops of both sides are a peaceloving lot (although I do wonder about the Paras and the Marines) and the news we listen for is that of peace moves, not damage inflicted on the enemy. That, we regard as unfortunately necessary because it is the only way to end this business, which our political masters have sent us into with such glee.

I must admit that I am disappointed in the actions of Dr Runcie [the Archbishop of Canterbury], both in stopping the Bishop of Argentina from coming to the Falklands to tell them that the Argentinians didn't actually have horns on their heads and in approving of this war in a 'St. George and the Dragon' way. But I suppose as he won an MC he thinks fighting for a just cause is OK. However, I am pleased to see that both the Liberals and the Baptists oppose war and advocate peaceful means. There are 'more ways to kill a cat than choking it with cream' and I believe that trade sanctions and world opinion should have been enough. It is not as if the Argentinians killed anyone, and now we have decided to go in heavy-handed about four hundred people are dead (including a hundred British) and it must have cost the UK about £1 billion so far (ships come out at about £150 million, planes, £10 million: people are cheaper). It will all end up with the equivalent of handing over a million pounds to each Falklander, and burning the money . . .

But enough of my sarcasm. They really should not send people in the Services to study history at university. The Captain, who is a very peaceloving and Christian man, and who has been in the Navy since the age of thirteen, just says things about democracy, and duty, and resisting invasion . . .

We seem to have settled into our way of life out here now, which isn't too different from normal. We still have hot water to wash in, copies of *Punch* to read, films, ample food, and a bed to sleep in at night. Much more comfortable than the poor old soldiers! One nice thing is that we sleep in our clothes so getting up in the morning is really easy! Paperwork has also subsided which is good. I spend quite a lot of time on watch on the Flight Deck which is very pleasant as I usually read a book, and look out over the sea at all the ships and the wildlife and enjoy the fresh air. The weather is just like the UK around here, and it is only just now starting to turn wintry. *Not* the huge gales that the press say there are.

We tend to live from day to day here and don't look too far ahead. In the first week of it all, when things were quite hot, people were very tense, and everyone lost a lot of weight. However, the UN peace negotiations brought a lull, when everybody adjusted to the situation. After that, most of the action was around the bridgehead, while we were out with the carriers. We have done quite a number of night raids and bombardments, but their aircraft haven't been flying at night, so that eases the adrenalin a bit. We don't like aircraft: especially the ones with the horrid missiles! . . .

Anyway, we are all looking forward to the Gurkhas doing their bit and clearing out the Argentinians from Stanley. Once the runway is in use again it will make life much easier. Stores can be flown in: air defence equipment and missiles, fighter planes, more troops, etc. Then it will just be question of mopping up resistance from the army, and keeping the Argentinian planes at a distance. The naval and air war could go on forever though, to some degree; until either they lose all their ships, submarines and planes or Galtieri & Co. get the boot. I'm sure someone will benefit from all this destruction, even though it is only Mrs Thatcher and the arms manufacturers!

. . . I'm glad to hear all about the news of your cottage and sailing; which reminds me, it's Summer, isn't it? See you when I get back, eventually.

To Christine   *HMS Glamorgan, 30 May 1982*

I received two lovely letters from you today dated 17 May – only 13 days, that's very quick . . . they came down with the QE2 . . .

. . . [F]or today and tomorrow, we have moved outside the [exclusion] zone to a holding area, where the tugs are also, incidentally. It is a very nice feeling to be out of it for a while – most relaxing . . .

It's now about midnight, and I have started to wake up. Because of our night-time usual activities we tend to be quite drowsy during the day and all awake at night! And if you go and have soup and bread at the watch change at 0200 hours you can stay awake quite happily until 0500 and not feel sleepy at all. Often when you are sleeping in short phases you can't remember whether it's day or night when you wake up. If the clock says 6 o'clock, for example, you have to think back to what the time was when you went to sleep, and then count forward. It's quite nice with three of us in the Flight Deck roster because it demands enough of your time to prevent you working set hours in the office. I usually turn up at 10 a.m. and work half an hour – even an hour some days! This gives you enough time off to spend as much time asleep as you like. Even when we are 'On Watch' we don't have to be on deck if nothing at all is happening. The sun rises here about 11 o'clock and sets about 8 p.m. (We are still on Greenwich Mean Time: much simpler all round.) So if I have the afternoon watch I often go out on deck to see the world, read a book, and take the air. It has started to get wintry now, and the wind is definitely cold . . . just like early December in Britain. The latitude here is about the same as London. It will be very odd having three Christmasses in the space of thirteen months.

We have some pet seagulls on the Flight Deck now. They are all white and look a bit like doves when flying . . . They have been following us around for about five days now. One is very friendly and eats bread out of the PO Aircrewman's hand and is quite jealous of his favoured position and sometimes chases the others away . . . The other seagull is a very pure white, but he hasn't quite mastered deck landings yet in a cross-wind. When he lands, he almost takes off again, and bounces around from leg to leg, stretching out very long toes to keep his balance: rather an inexperienced pilot, though. I often feel he needs tying down with the nylon lashings, like the helicopter, to keep him on deck. He is a bit more timid than the other, but quite happily eats the bread we leave out for him. They are usually both to be seen strutting round the Flight Deck, pecking at this and that, and investigating all the corners and cosy holes. They haven't yet started nesting in the hangar!

We have been hearing recently on the News of 2 Battalion Parachute Regiment's brilliant attack on Darwin and Goose Green. This must rate as one of the most outstanding infantry actions in history – on a par with Clive at Plassey. Attacking at odds of one to three, when it should have been three to one . . . is utterly incredible. It must have been a dreadfully fierce battle with 250 Argentine dead. I hope the Argentinians' willingness to fight and accept such losses makes the press at home treat them with more respect. As ever, those furthest from the front jeer and jibe the loudest, have the most bravado, and urge war the most . . .

Last time I wrote we had just moved to the maintenance area for 48 hours: and we are still here a week later! All our maintenance has been done but we have organised a nice little niche for ourselves here, in managing all the supply ships, getting them in the right station, organising whom and from whom they should fuel, delivering their mail and stores to them with helicopters, etc. We've even conned the Admiral so well that although our helicopter isn't working we have borrowed another ship's; and do their stores transfers with it. We are now known as RFA* *Glamorgan*.

The area out here, well to the east of the carrier group, is known as the TRALA (something like 'Tug [or Transit?], Repair, and Logistics Area') and very tra-la-la- it is too. We haven't been to action stations all week and at night don't even bother with defence watches. It has been a great tonic for everyone, especially for those who had been working straight one-in-two watches (i.e. on-off, on-off) for the whole of [this] last month and the last part of April. Life has returned to the Wardroom, people are smiling and making jokes, reading the papers and watching the film in the evening. Usually, the Wardroom is deserted except for meal times, when everyone is changing watches, and the only people you'll find there are layabout Flight Deck Officers. However, I'm disturbed that some of the junior ratings and single officers actually want to go back in the [operational] area (I shall have to suppress these mutinous tendencies).

Actually, the Fleet down here has changed quite a lot and there are only a few of the old hands left . . . just to give you an idea, this is what has happened to the original Fleet:

Hermes/Invincible:	Both still in the [operational] area
Glamorgan:	TRALA area
Antrim:	South Georgia; undergoing repairs from D-day damage
Glasgow:	Returning to UK after unexploded bomb damage
Sheffield:	Sunk on 4 May
Coventry:	Sunk on 25 May
Broadsword/Brilliant:	Both still in area: both damaged and will need repairs in UK (in time)
Arrow:	In San Carlos Bay: will need to return to UK: split hull from *Sheffield* knocking [into her]
Alacrity:	Returning to UK; mechanical problems

* Royal Fleet Auxiliary (the merchant ships of the Royal Navy).

| *Plymouth/Yarmouth:* | Both in San Carlos Bay: will need to return for maintenance in UK |

And also the first wave of replacements:

Argonaut:	Returning to UK: bomb damage
Ardent:	Sunk 21 May
Antelope:	Sunk 21 May

– which is why we don't have first call on returning to UK . . .

There was a report in the press on about 2 June saying that *Glamorgan* would be returning first because of bomb damage – total fabrication. *Antrim* is the one damaged by the bomb. They are dreadful, the press: they just make these things up when they haven't got solid facts to work on – like the *Sunday Times* account of the Pebble Island [raid] which said 'This is what it was probably like' – and then gave graphic detail – all of which was wrong. Anyway I know these press reports must be horribly alarming but they are just not true. The most blatant one is the weather, which they say is foul, but which is much better than UK.

I don't like writing about the war to you but just for the record I suppose I should let you know what we did so you aren't fed untrue tit-bits.

1 May:	Shelled Stanley airport with *Arrow* amd *Alacrity*, close inshore, inside the minefield – during daylight. Attacked by eight Mirages – low, and only seen at a mile; bombs dropped near the stern lifting the ship out of the water; rockets fired down the side of the ship; cannon fire. No damage done . . . Returned at night to shell the airport again (aircraft could not fly at night).
2 May:	Argentine pincer naval attack: northern group of two corvettes to decoy British ships from main group and attack them during day. We were surface group commander, but were [sent] south to shell Stanley again and helicopters sank the corvettes with Sea Skua during the night (and *Belgrano* sank to the south). Consequently, we were not required.
4 May:	*Sheffield* sunk in main group: nobody else knew she had been hit until an hour later (she lost all communications). A worrying time.
6 and 8 May:	Bombarding Stanley again at night (1–12 May, action stations frequently, about three times per day).

133

6–21 May:	UN talks, and lessening of activity in the area.
14 May:	Pebble Island raid with *Hermes*. We destroyed eight aircraft by gunfire. The SAS took out an ammunition dump (huge orange glow in the night) and three aircraft with plastic explosives. A very moonlit night – jumpy. High-speed escape from 08.30: all engines flat out. The ship's wake was as broad as a motorway!
16, 18, 19, 20 May:	Bombarding Stanley again at night: *their* shells landed 200 yards away. Final night, we dropped scare charges and illuminated ourselves with flares – we scared ourselves more then the Argentinians.
21 May:	D-Day. Because of the daily bombardment we were not put into the area. All the ships were hit: two sunk and two written off, a dreadful day, as we heard the news coming in. We would have been in *Antrim*'s place had not the Admiral transferred to us before Ascension, and *Antrim* had gone to South Georgia. *Antrim* was bombed and strafed. Evening of 21 May: we were ordered into the area to replace *Antrim*: an awful couple of hours before the Admiral changed his mind and decided that he couldn't afford to lose any more ships. *Coventry* was ordered in instead, to a different, more open sea area, to act as a 'Missile Trap' and was of course sunk four days later.
25 May:	(*Coventry* sunk inshore) An Exocet attack with about five seconds warning. *Atlantic Conveyor*, the biggest ship in the force, sunk. We bombarded Stanley again that night in retaliation, and launched our Seaslug at the runway (they don't go off on the surface: it is just a gesture).
26, 28 May:	Night bombardment again with *Ambuscade* and *Avenger*. Shells fell to fifty yards of us. We launched two more Seaslugs. Frightened us more than them. We have now fired 1,000 4.5″ shells.
30 May:	Exocet attack again. Forty-five seconds warning this time, and we got into position (bows towards missile) and fired chaff . . . However, missile came towards us and we braced for impact. Missile either went into a wave, or into some chaff,

or ran out of gas, quarter of a mile from us. Phew!!

30 May: Full speed ahead for the TRALA: and here we are.

Over this period, the mood and feeling on board have changed from being very tense to becoming used to the situation. The attacks are not particularly frightening, they are over so quickly. However, one always has to be prepared to go to Action Stations and to expect this and that: and that is the main difference to life. It is an odd feeling being attacked; a mixture of 'Goodbye, cruel world', as you lie there with tin helmet on, braced for it: and a feeling that 'They must be mad. Don't they know it's very unsafe shooting things at other people?' One is always so conscious of safety, normally, you just cannot imagine somebody doing something as deliberately unsafe as pointing it at anyone – and pressing the button. The best thing to do is to have a few wets before an attack. I'd had a drink before the Exocet attack and the pulse rate stayed very normal, although when 'Brace, Brace, Brace' came over the broadcast I did think to myself 'Expletive deleted'. They had it worst in the Ops Room where they could see it coming towards us – the Ops Officer said his heart almost pounded itself out of its rib cage. Poor man: ignorance is bliss on these occasions.

Now, of course, the mood on board is very relaxed, and very nice it is too. We have just gone back to '1 in 4', cruising watches. Living day to day, one tries to make times when everything is going very well indeed – like when coming off watch in the evening, when nothing is planned for the night, or when some mail has come and there's a Mars Bar saved up to eat, or just when there's no work looming and some time to read a book; when the Falklands are disappearing behind us at a great rate of knots after a raid, or when we are out of the way in the TRALA. In such times I feel a sense of 'well being', as now when I've just had a Mars Bar and am writing to you.

These times are getting more frequent now that we're out here with the supply ships, and it is nice to have them; easier to do living on a day to day basis, when it's just the present that is important – and the present's OK. In the same way one looks forward to meal times, and having a beer, and that sort of thing: the sort of thing one just accepts, normally, and concentrates on the horrid part of life, i.e. work!

One of our jobs out here is to transfer stores around between ships and yesterday I walked into the hangar and found a nuclear bomb there. I suppose if the USA and USSR have got 7,000 each, the chance of walking into one must be increased, but nevertheless

135

I was rather surprised, and wondered if it was worth sheltering in the hangar any more. Of course, it turned out to be a drill round, full of concrete, that *Fort Austin*, now eventually going home, was taking back to England. I don't really know why we brought any down here. Loosing one off really would evaporate support for us by the EEC and Third World. Anyway, at least this lump of concrete is going back.

To H and E   *HMS Glamorgan, 8 June 1982*
[received 30 June]

It seems quite some time since I wrote to you last; I have now received your letters up to 17 May. Thank you very much for them. It is very nice indeed to hear news of the normal world as one has to look very hard in the papers to find anything that is not about war.

. . . Life is very nicely routine here, and everybody is very relaxed and very well. We recently had first crack at a store ship straight out from England, so we are all topped up with food and goodies. We have ice-cream for lunch and have even had some apples . . .

Lots of love for now; I will write again soon.

HMS GLAMORGAN

Killed in Action, 12 June 1982
Michael Adcock, Petty Officer, aged 34
Brian Easton, Cook, aged 24
Mark Henderson, Air Engineering mechanic, aged 20
Brian Hinge, Air Engineering Mechanic, aged 24
David Lee, Acting Chief Engineering Mechanic, aged 35
Kelvin McCallum, Air Engineering Artificer, aged 27
Brian Malcolm, Cook, aged 22
Terry Perkins, Marine Engineering Mechanic, aged 19
Mark Sambles, Leading Cook, aged 29
Tony Sillence, Leading Cook, aged 26
John Stroud, Steward, aged 20
David Tinker, Lieutenant, aged 25
Colin Vickers, Petty Officer, aged 33

Committed to the ocean deep in position 51° 50′ 50″ South,

53° 31′ 80″ West, 160 miles East of Falklands Islands: on the evening of 12 June.

Now that you have read the extracts you may want to extend your reading into talking and writing. The suggestions that follow can be done on your own, with a partner or in groups. The activities range from suggestions based on the extracts to opportunities for a personal and imaginative response. Most of the extracts are about real people's lives and in some cases may be upsetting. Nevertheless, reading them and thinking seriously about the issues that they raise may still be a positive experience. It may also encourage you to see writing as something more than a school exercise and inspire you to write for yourself.

The Magic Apple Tree *by Susan Hill*

Starting points

1 Having read what Susan Hill has to say about the place where she lives, talk about it in pairs or small groups. List everything you have learnt about Barley, the people who live there and their lifestyle. Draw a plan or map of the village.

2 Whether you live in a city, town, village or hamlet you probably belong to a community. If you live in a city or town, your community may be just your street or estate; if you live in a small village, it might include everyone. You might belong to a larger community of people who do not all live close by but get together for social events and to celebrate special occasions, e.g. engagements, weddings, festivals.

    In pairs or small groups, talk about your community and list all its features: where is it based? how many people does it include? what sort of activities and events does it share? You may want to use your list as the starting point for a piece of written work about where you live. *Or* you may want to draw a map or plan showing the main features.

3 Susan Hill's community is based upon the village of Barley and many of its activities focus on the church and its calendar of events. Because it is in the country, the seasons and weather play a large part in village life.

    In pairs or small groups, draw up a calendar for your community showing the activities and when they take place. It could take the form of a chart, a timeline or a circular diagram.

4 As a writer, Susan Hill is particularly good at descriptions of people,

places and events. She manages to make her readers feel that they are there, sharing the excitement and the atmosphere. Look again at her writing and try to analyse how she achieves this effect. Look at the details she provides, the words she uses, the lengths of sentences. Try to use some of these techniques in your own descriptive writing.

Talking
Read what Susan Hill says about hunting (pp. 6–7) The rights and wrongs of hunting is a very topical issue. At a recent AGM, the National Trust debated the resolution to prohibit: 'all fox, deer and hare hunting with hounds on land owned, leased and rented, unless legally bound to allow such activities by existing tenancies, leases, or deed of gift.' Imagine you are members of the National Trust and debate that resolution.

For a formal debate you need:
- a motion or resolution for debate – a statement which those listening will vote on at the end to say whether they agree or disagree with it. (Use the one provided above.)

- a Chair who organises and controls the proceedings and to whom all comments are addressed

- a proposer who speaks first and supports the motion, putting forward the arguments as to why the House should support it

- an opposer who speaks second and puts forward the counter arguments as to why the House should not support the motion

- a seconder for the motion who speaks third and supports the main speaker.

- a seconder against the motion who speaks fourth and supports the opposer.

After the Chair has introduced the four main speakers and they have put their cases, the debate is thrown open to the Floor for the House to ask questions of the speakers or to make comments. Before voting on the motion, the Chair asks the proposer and opposer to sum up.

At the AGM of the National Trust the motion was defeated.

Media work
1 Listen to the radio 4 programme *Down Your Way* in which celebrities take the listeners on a tour of where they live, describing the main features of the place and speaking to the local inhabitants. In groups, imagine that you are the production team for that programme and that you have been sent to Barley to direct Susan Hill in an edition of the programme.

Using the information in the extracts, you will have to decide what is to go in the programme and who is to appear in it with Susan Hill. Then you will need to script it with different members of the group taking different parts. You can either record it or perform it to the rest of the class.

2 On page 3, Susan Hill talks about an emergency local radio station that was set up to broadcast news and weather information during the heavy snow and how important those broadcasts were in supporting the community. In pairs, devise a day's programme of events for that local radio station in that situation. Script two of the items you record or perform them to the rest of the class.

3 Read again about the death of Miss Ivy Moor (p. 10). Write the newspaper report that would have appeared in the local newspaper.

4 You have been asked to interview the Hon. Claudia Hay for an article in either a magazine called *Working Woman* or a magazine called *Farming Today*. Before you write your article, you need to think about the kind of magazine each of them is and what sort of articles they would feature. Give a brief descripton of the magazine as an introduction to your article.

5 You have been asked to write an article about Barley in a travel book that is featuring a section on English villages. You will need three pictures to illustrate your article. Draw or describe them.

6 In small groups, design and write a pamphlet for an animal rights group to use in its campaign to get hunting banned.

7 Write an article for a teenage magazine on the increase in vegetarianism, particularly among young people.

Writing

1 Descriptions of the seasons play a large part in Susan Hill's book. Describe your favourite season. You may want to write it as a poem or a list, e.g. Spring is . . .

2 Keep your own nature journal. It could cover a short period like a week and focus on something specific, like the birds that visit your garden. You may prefer to cover a longer period of time and a wider area. You could illustrate your journal with photographs or sketches.

3 Every community has its *characters*. Susan Hill writes about Nance and George, Miss Moor, the Twomeys and the Hon. Claudia Hay. Choose two or more characters you know and describe them in detail.

Personal response

1 Reading these extracts may have triggered off memories from your own life of Christmas, Bonfire night, bad weather, people you have known, special moments. Write about them as chapters of your autobiography.

2 Her house and the village are obviously special places for Susan Hill. Describe your favourite place. It does not have to be where you live, it could be where you would like to live or somewhere you have been on holiday.

Further ideas

1 Susan Hill has written a number of books, radio scripts, short stories and stories for children. She has also written another autobiographi-

cal book called *Family*. She reviews books and often appears on radio and television on literary programmes. You may be interested in reading more of her work and making a special study of it. Here are some suggestions of books and stories for you to try:

The Woman in Black (Longman Imprint Book, 1989)
'The Badness Within Him' in *Frankie Mae and other stories* (Nelson, 'Responses' series; 1987)
Strange Meeting (Penguin, 1974)
In the Springtime of the Year (Penguin, 1977)

2 You could make a special study of nature journals. Read two or three and compare and contrast them. Here are some suggestions:

Selections from the Diary of the Rev. Francis Kilvert (Jonathan Cape)
The Diary of a Farmer's Wife: 1796–1797, Anne Hughes (Penguin, 1980)
The Country Diary of an Edwardian Lady, Edith Holden (Michael Joseph Ltd., 1977)

3 Many writers have written about their lives in the country, mostly about growing up there. You could read some of these accounts and then write about growing up in the country, comparing it with your own upbringing. Here are some suggestions:

Never No More, Maura Laverty (Students' Virago, 1988)
Cider With Rosie, Laurie Lee (Penguin)
Country World: Memories of Childhood, Alison Uttley, selected by Lucy Meredith (Faber and Faber, 1986)

4 For an interesting comparison of life in a village with life in a busy town, read:

Whole of a Morning Sky, Grace Nichols (Virago, 1986)

English Journey *by Beryl Bainbridge*

Starting points

1 In pairs or small groups, make a list of the places Beryl Bainbridge visits in these extracts. With the aid of an atlas, draw a map of Britain and mark her route on it. Also mark on it where you live.

2 In her introduction, Beryl Bainbridge says that she was not an objective traveller; she allows her own personal opinions to show through. In pairs, make a list of the things that you have learnt about Beryl Bainbridge and her views. What does she like and dislike? How does she show this in her writing?

3 Imagine that Beryl Bainbridge is to visit your area. In pairs or small groups, make a list of the places that you think she would visit. Choose one of those places and describe it as you see it. Then try to describe it as if you were Beryl Bainbridge.

Talking

Imagine that you have been asked to give an illustrated talk on your area, past and present, to the Local History Society. First of all, you will need to decide what you are going to focus on, e.g. buildings, work places and jobs, housing, the life-style of people, schools. Then you will need to do some research.

You can get information from a variety of sources: the local library, a local museum and local people who have lived in the area for a long time, your grandparents, perhaps. If you are going to interview people, it is a good idea to draw up a list of questions first. It can also be helpful to tape record the interview as a way of keeping track of the answers. As part of your research, you will also need to look for old photographs, slides, pictures or maps.

Once you have assembled all your material, you will need to plan out your talk, deciding at what point and how you are going to use the illustrations. You could also use extracts from any taped interviews that you have made.

Media work

1 Reread the brief account of the young woman in the 1890s who jumped off Clifton Suspension Bridge and lived to be eighty (p. 21). Invent a story to explain who she was and why she jumped. Write a story for the local paper, *The Clifton Gazette*, reporting fully on the incident.

2 *English Journey* was made into a series of television documentaries. Choose any one of the places included in these extracts and, using the storyboard format provided below, depict the scene as you would produce it.

TV storyboard

Camera instructions to camera operator – close-up, long shot, mid shot, zoom in or away.

Visuals use these frames to show what the viewer will see.

Sounds words or sound effects

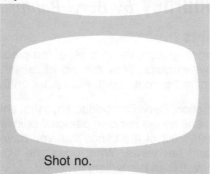

Shot no.

3 You have been asked to interview Beryl Bainbridge about her travels for an article in a teenage magazine. You have been asked to focus particulary on her impressions of the effects on young people of unemployment and modern developments. You may also want to

focus on her account of meeting Bing and his friends (pp. 31–33), One way of organising your article would be to use a question and answer format.

4 If possible, watch the television programme *Treasure Hunt*. In small groups, discuss the format and list what happens. Using your own area, devise a treasure hunt with clues and maps. The area you choose does not have to be extensive – it would be possible to devise a treasure hunt based on your school and its grounds.

5 Tourism is expanding and most places have realised that they have something worth seeing and promoting. Many places produce pamphlets, maps or guides listing the places of interest in their area.

Working in small groups, plan, design and produce a publication listing the features of interest in your area. Before you start, you might find it helpful to look at examples of leaflets that have been professionally produced. You can pick them up free in most tourist information centres or travel agents.

6 Reread Beryl Bainbridge's descriptions of the Cotswolds (pp. 22–24). Imagine that you are the tourist development officer for the Cotswolds. You have to plan a campaign to promote the area. Decide what you will need to produce: inserts in holiday brochures, posters, advertisements, maps and guides, car stickers, badges. Before you start to design these materials, you need to decide who they are going to be aimed at and what image of the place you are going to promote. Remember that you are trying to persuade people to visit the area.

Writing
Travel writing can take many forms from diaries and journals to letters and entire books. The journeys can be to ordinary or exotic places or indeed to imaginary places. The important feature about all travel writing is that it should be able to conjure up for the reader the essence of the place. This is achieved by close observation and description of the place itself, the buildings, the people, the atmosphere, the weather – whatever the writer chooses to focus on to make it real for the reader.

Try your hand at travel writing: choose a journey – your most recent holiday, your journey to school or to an imaginary island. Once you have chosen your journey, decide on the format that you think would suit it best.

Personal response
1 Beryl Bainbridge has much to say about work and unemployment, modern developments and housing, the North–South divide and people's lives. She was writing in 1983. Imagine that you have been asked to take part in a survey to find out what young people think about these issues today. Write a personal account of your views on what it is like being young at this time. What have you got to look forward to? What are your employment prospects? What do you think about pollution? What sort of society do you live in? Are you happy with it?

143

2 Much of what Beryl Bainbridge writes about is conerned with the past and the 'good old days'. Imagine you are sixty years old and you are looking back on the time when you were fifteen. Write about what you think you would remember and miss. This could be written as a diary entry.

Further ideas

1 You might want to do an extended study on travel writing, comparing and contrasting styles and techniques. Some books to consider include:

> *Gulliver's Travels*, Jonathan Swift (Penguin)
> *Tour Through The Whole Island of Great Britain*, Daniel Defoe, (Penguin)
> *The Kingdom By The Sea*, Paul Theroux (Hamish Hamilton)
> *Traveller's Prelude*, Freya Stark (Century)
> *Journeys in Persia and Kurdistan*, Isabella Bird (Virago)
> *A Short Walk in the Hindu Kush*, Eric Newby (Picador)

2 Read J.B. Priestley's *English Journey*. Compare and contrast it with Beryl Bainbridge's.

3 Ray Bradbury is a famous science fiction writer. Many of his stories would, perhaps, be better described as futuristic as they are concerned with events in the future. Two of his stories link well with the theme of travel and some of the issues raised in Beryl Bainbridge's writing. Read 'The Pedestrian' and 'The Sound of Thunder' in *The Golden Apples of the Sun* (Corgi). Write your own story about time travel or a future society.

Joanne's Diary *by Joanne Gillespie*

It is very difficult suggesting ideas for work on this extract because Joanne is a real person fighting for her life. The suggestions are intended to help you reflect upon what you have read.

Starting points

In small groups, make a list of the things that kept Joanne going. What strategies does she use to keep on fighting? What have you learnt about her from reading about her struggle to overcome her illness?

Talking

Role-play a committee meeting of a hospital board to discuss whether parents should be allowed to stay with their child all the time during the child's stay in hospital. You will need representatives from all the interested bodies: doctors, nurses, parents, hospital administrators.

Before you start, you will need to work out what the relevant issues are. Some of the things you will need to consider are: the welfare of the children, the facilities needed and what is actually available, the cost of the parents' accommodation and meals, any rules and regulations that will be required, the need for an age limit and so on.

Media work

1 Write an article about Joanne for the local newspaper. Think up a suitable headline.

2 In pairs, work out an interview with Joanne for local radio. Script it.

3 Write an article about Joanne for a magazine called *Here's Health*. Focus on her use of alternative medicine.

Writing

1 You have been asked to nominate Joanne for a Children of Courage Award. Write a letter of recommendation to the selection committee. (Joanne was actually presented with her Children of Courage Award on December 14th 1988.)

2 In her introduction, Joanne says that she wrote her book because when she was ill and bewildered there was nothing written for children to help them. In small groups, design and write a pamphlet for small children to prepare them for a stay in hospital. Write an accompanying leaflet for parents.

3 Imagine that you are a schoolfriend of Joanne's. Write some entries in your diary in which you comment on Joanne's illness and your feelings and reactions.

Personal response

1 One of the issues that Joanne touches upon is whether people, particularly children, should be told the truth about serious issues like illness and death. Write about a time when you had to face the truth about a difficult and painful situation, perhaps, after the truth had been hidden from you.

2 Reading the extract may have triggered off memories from your own childhood of being ill and being frightened, or of going to hospital, or being brave, or facing up to something difficult. Write an extract for your autobiography focusing on any one of these experiences.

Further ideas

Joanne's diary focuses on bravery in the face of illness. There are other accounts of extreme bravery by young girls. You may want to do an extended study on heroines – real and fictional. You might like to begin by doing some research on the life of Flora Macdonald or Grace Darling. Here are some other suggestions for further reading:

The Diary of Anne Frank, Anne Frank (Longmans Imprint)
Points of Departure, edited by Jane Browne (Students' Virago)
Words by Heart, Ouida Sebestyen (Hamish Hamilton)

Sarah's Letters *by 'Sarah'*

Starting points

Working in small groups, you are going to compile a dossier on Sarah based on the information that is revealed in her letters. Before you start, you will need to decide how best to tackle the task. Perhaps the group could split up into twos and each pair could focus on a different aspect: home and family, school, friends, personality and appearance. Once you have gathered all the information, you will need to think of the best way of presenting it. Keep the dossier safe, you will need to refer to it for other activities.

Talking

1 Role-play a meeting at the grammar school between Sarah's parents, her form teacher and her year head to discuss her lack of progress.

2 Sarah believed that because her first secondary school was single sex that it added to her problems of shyness by making it very difficult for her to mix with boys. There are some people who believe that single sex schools are better for girls because they enable them to achieve more. There are other people who believe that girls should be educated separately for religious reasons.

Imagine that in your area the Education Authority has decided to close down its single sex schools in favour of mixed schools. Have a public meeting to discuss the issue. It should involve all the class and you will need to sort out in advance who is going to chair the meeting and who is going to represent all the interested bodies.

Media work

1 One of Sarah's letters that is not included here was very critical of her grammar school. With her permission the letter was printed as an article in the school magazine of her new school. *Either* write the article, using the information given in other letters to help you, *or* write an article about your own school experiences.

2 Consider some of Sarah's problems: unhappy at school, unable to get on with boys, a particular problem with Richard, ill at ease with other people, feeling vulnerable, easily hurt and upset by others. In pairs, choose some of those concerns and, taking it in turns, write letters about them to a problem or advice page in a teenage magazine and write the replies.

Writing

1 Using your dossier to help you, write three school reports on Sarah: one from her primary school, one from her grammar school and one from her comprehensive school.

2 Sarah says in one of her letters that she kept a diary throughout this period. Write some entries in that diary, covering a span of time and a number of incidents.

3 Sarah is now grown up. Write an account of what you think she is like now and what her life is like. You could write it in the first person or as a description.

Personal response

1 In one of her letters Sarah talks about having invented a friend when she was a small child. Small children quite often do this. If you had

an imaginary friend or brother or sister, write about your memories of that time.

2 Reading Sarah's letters, particularly her accounts of playing out and the neighbours in her old neighbourhood, moving house and moving school, may have triggered memories of similar incidents in your own life. Write about them as chapters in your autobiography.

3 Write about growing up and the problems that you face. You may want to write this as a poem, as a private letter or as a diary entry.

4 Sarah writes very honestly about herself. In her letters, she is trying hard to understand herself and what makes her the way she is. Write your own self-portrait in which you try to analyse yourself closely.

Catherine's Diary *by Catherine Dunbar*

Of all the material in the book this is probably the most upsetting and difficult to deal with. Catherine was a real person who, unlike Sarah and Joanne, was not successful in her struggle to come to terms with life and to understand herself. At the age of twenty-two, she died of starvation in considerable pain, defeated by her illness, anorexia nervosa.

Thames Television's Education Department made a film about Catherine based on the book written by her mother from which these extracts from Catherine's diary were taken. It is a very powerful and moving film.

Writing
1 Catherine's mother wrote her book as a testament to a much-loved daughter and in the hope that it would help other families facing the same dilemma. Write an article for a teenage magazine about Catherine and her illness.

2 Imagine that you were a friend of Catherine. Write about your feelings and response to her illness and death. You may want to write it as a letter to someone, as a diary entry or as a descriptive account.

The Diary of a Teenage Health Freak *by* 'Pete Payne'

Starting points
1 Using the same format as the one Pete Payne uses, write a profile of yourself, your family and friends.

2 In groups, talk about what you have read as preparation for writing a review of the book. The idea behind the book was to give teenagers information about health matters in an interesting and amusing way

Do you think it works? Did you find it helpful and interesting? Would you have rather read a more straightforward, factual book?

Talking

1 The opening extracts are about family rows: rows between parents and children, between brothers and sisters and between parents. Either improvise or script and act out a family row.

2 As a class, imagine that you are the invited audience at a television chat show dealing with divorce and its effects on children. Choose someone to be the compere and devise a number of questions that you will consider.

Media work

1 Read about depression on pages 85–86 and, using the information included there, devise a personality quiz for readers of a teenage magazine so that they can work out if they are depressed. Here are some ideas to start you off:

FED UP OR DEPRESSED?

Complete our quiz to find out how fed up you REALLY are.

Read the questions, choose your answer, **a**, **b** or **c**, add up your score (answers at the bottom of the page) and read what our experts have to say about you from your score.

1. When you wake up in the morning do you feel:
a) tired
b) energetic
c) anxious

2. Do you have trouble sleeping:
a) never
b) rarely
c) frequently

---

2 Reread the section about alcohol (pp. 92–94) and write an article for a teenage magazine about the problems of teenage drinking.

3 Imagine that *The Diary of a Teenage Health Freak* is being adapted for television. Choose an incident from the extracts that you think would make a good episode. Using the storyboard format provided on page 142, depict the scene as you would produce it.

Writing

1 Part of the Education Reform Act states that governing bodies have a legal obligation to decide a policy on sex education for their schools. Some schools already have an extensive programme of personal and social development which includes sex education. In drawing up their policies, governors are having to start by deciding whether this is a topic that should be taught in schools. Some people think not: they think it is a matter best left to parents and dealt with

at home. If it is to be taught in school, the following questions need to be considered: what should it be taught? to whom? by whom? how? when?

Imagine that you have been asked by the governing body of your school to write a report for them reflecting the views of your class on this issue. In order to write your report, you will need to get the opinions of your classmates either by interviewing them or by devising a questionnaire for them to complete. Once you have completed your research, you will need to think about the best way of organising and presenting your report.

2 In small groups, you are going to plan a party to celebrate your sixteenth birthday. You will need to start by thinking about what makes a good party. Then you will need to consider the time and place, guest list and invitations, food and drink, music and other organisational points like how to avoid gate-crashers. What would your parents attitude be? How would you get them to co-operate?

Once you have planned your party, use the experience you have gained to write a handbook for young people on organising a party.

3 Despite the statistics to prove the health risks associated with smoking, young people still smoke. There is even an increase in the numbers of young women smoking. You have been asked to help devise an advertising campaign aimed at young people, warning them of the dangers of smoking. In small groups, plan your campaign: consider what material you would need to design and write – pamphlets, stickers, badges, advertisements for the radio and television, posters, a slogan. Remember that you are trying to be informative and dissuade young people from smoking.

Personal response

1 Write a story that may be based on your own experience called 'The Party'.

2 Write about a time when you have been depressed or anxious.

3 Write a few pages of your own humorous diary either basing it on your family and life or inventing the characters.

Further ideas

1 Fictional diaries are a very popular literary form and you may want to do an extended study of them. Here are some suggestions for further study:

The Secret Diary of Adrian Mole Aged 13¾, Sue Townsend (Macmillan)

The Diary of a Nobody, George and Weedon Grossmith (Penguin, 1965)

The Amazing and Death-Defying Diary of Eugene Dingman, Paul Zindel (Bodley Head)

French Letters: The Life and Loves of Miss Maxine Harrison, Form 4a, Eileen Fairweather (Women's Press)

2 Maureen Stewart is an author who uses the diary form and letters

as a way of writing stories for young people that are concerned with important issues. *Vicki's Habit* (Puffin Plus) is about the traumas of teenage alcoholism and is written as a fictional account of letters and reports between Vicki and Mr Jones, the school counsellor. *Dear Emily* is the correspondence between Maria who lives in the big city and her penfriend Emily who lives in the country. There is also a sequel called *Love From Greg*. Both are published by Puffin. You could do an extended study of Maureen Stewart and consider why she uses these forms to write her stories.

French Letters *by 'Maxine Harrison'*

Starting points

In small groups, pool all the information you have about Maxine and then write a profile of her, her family and friends.

Talking

1 On page 115, Maxine asks Jean to write or ring as soon as she gets the letter. In pairs, improvise the phone call that you think would have taken place.

2 Maxine is not looking forward to taking French Jean home for tea. Taking friends home for tea to meet the family can be a difficult and embarrassing occasion. In small groups, improvise or script and act out a family scene in which you are taking a boyfriend or girlfriend home for tea for the first time.

Media work

1 Maxine does not choose very well when she buys her new clothes in readiness for French Jean's visit. Imagine you are the Fashion Editor for a teenage magazine and you are putting together a feature on buying clothes on a budget for a sight-seeing holiday in a big city. Your feature can be aimed at boys or girls or both. As well as offering concrete suggestions, you will need to provide advice for your readers on how to choose clothes that will suit them.

You will need to illustrate your article. Use pictures cut out of other magazines and catalogues or your own drawings and sketches. Design the clothes yourself if you like. You will also need to think about page design and layout and headlines. Look at the fashion pages of some magazines to give you some ideas before you start.

2 Instead of writing to Jean, Maxine could have written for advice to the problem page of a magazine. In pairs, write a letter from Maxine to a problem page asking for advice on any of the things that bother her. Write the reply.

3 Imagine that *French Letters* is being adapted for broadcasting on the radio. In small groups, choose any incident from the extracts and write the radio script giving full details about sound effects and guidance for the actors reading the parts. Record or perform your script for the rest of the class.

4 Adapt the story of Maxine and her French penfriend's visit to tell as a picture story in a magazine of love stories. You will need to decide how many frames you will require and what will go in each frame. You can draw it or describe it. Speech can either be as bubbles coming out the characters' mouths or written at the bottom of each picture frame.

Writing
1 Imagine you have a penfriend. Write your first letter to them telling them all about yourself. You may want to include some photographs or drawings or postcards.

2 Imagine your penfriend is coming to stay with you for a week. Plan the week's activities. You may want to refer back to the work you did on *English Journey* for places to visit and things to do in your area.

3 Money, or the lack of it, is a common problem for young people. Conduct a survey in your class on money matters to find out how much money your classmates have, what they spend it on, who gives it to them, their jobs and how much they earn. You will need to think up appropriate questions to get the information you want.

Once you have conducted your survey you will need to write up the results as a report. You will need to think about the best way to do that: as a wall chart, as a written report with diagrams, as a graph or chart.

4 We only see Maxine's letters but in places she refers to Jean's letters. Write some of Jean's letters to Maxine.

5 At the end of the book, Maxine goes on a date with Frankie, Imelda's older brother. Write the letter Maxine would have written to Jean telling her all about it.

6 Write an entry in Maxine's diary describing her feelings the day after French Jean had gone home.

Personal response
1 Write about your best friend. You may choose to write about someone from your past or your present.

2 Reading this extract might have triggered off memories from your own life of moving, problems at school, worries about relationships, your family, job experiences – choose any of these and write some chapters of your autobiography.

3 Write a story or poem about the first experience of falling in love.

A Message from The Falklands *by David Tinker*

This is another extract that needs sensitive handling. David Tinker was a real person who was killed in action at the age of twenty-five, fighting in a war that he had come to believe was futile.

Talking and writing

1 The Falklands War was a recent major historical event. Talk to older people – your teachers, your parents, neighbours – to find out what they remember about it. When did they hear about it? How did they feel about it? Did they think that it was right that Britain should go to war with Argentina over the Falkland Islands?

2 In small groups, draw up a time chart of the events in the war using the information provided here. In order to complete the chart, you will need to find out when the Falklands War ended and how the situation was resolved. Design the chart so that you leave space to fill in – perhaps in a different colour – where David Tinker was and when.

3 Imagine you are a war correspondent for Radio News. In pairs, work out two interviews with David Tinker. The first interview should be in April, The second interview should be at the end of May. The interviews should try to show the change in his attitude to the war, to the Argentinians, to the Prime Minister, Mrs Thatcher and the government. You could choose to do this as a written activity and write the interviews as newspaper reports.

4 *A Message from the Falklands* has been turned into a play. Choose any section from the extract and adapt it as a play. Script it with full directions for the actors and any other information about the stage set and props that you think are necessary. Perform your scene to the rest of the class.

5 In one of his letters, David Tinker says a boy's upbringing is centred on warlike activities and war stories. Do you think that is as true today? What is a girl's upbringing likely to be centred on?

6 Write a story or poem about separation.

7 There are many references in the letters to the media and their coverage of the war and how they often got information wrong and gave a false impression. Try to get hold of some back copies of newspapers at the time of the war and read their reports. Did they all agree about whether Britain should be fighting the war? Did they all give the same information? Did they paint an accurate picture of what was going on, do you think?

8 You could do an extended study on the coverage of the Falklands War in other writing, comparing and contrasting the way the subject is dealt with. Here are some suggestions for further reading:
> 'Three Weeks to Argentina', a poem by Gavin Ewart in *Wordlife*, Richard Knott (Nelson, 'Responses' series, 1988)
> *Coasting* (the third section onwards is about the Falklands), Jonathan Raban (Collins Harvill, 1986)
> *The Battle for the Falklands*, Max Hastings and Simon Jenkins
> *On Foreign Ground*, Eduardo Quiroga (Andre Deutsch)

9 Choose one of the following activities:

- read some war poetry from the First and Second World Wars and compare and contrast attitudes to war
- compile your own anthology of war poems.

You may like to look at the work the poets listed here. All these poets have written about experiences and attitudes to war:
Siegfried Sassoon   Wilfred Owen   Jessie Pope   Charles Causley
John Bayliss   Mary Gabrielle Collins   Randall Jarrell   Olivia Fitzroy
Karen Gershon   Rupert Brooke
Prepare a dramatised reading on the theme of war.

Further uses of diaries, journals and letters

As well as being a source of pleasure and interest, diaries, journals and letters can be very useful ways of writing. Here are some suggestions.

1 As Sarah and Pete say in their extracts, writing helped them to sort out how they felt and enabled them to come to a better understanding of people and events in their lives. This kind of private and reflective writing can be very good therapy but you need to decide for yourself how private you want it to be. Sarah initially wrote her letters to her English teacher, but she gave permission for one of them to be published in the school magazine, and much later she gave permission for them to be published in a book. Catherine's diary was never intended for publication but, after her death, her mother decided to publish it to help others. Joanne's diary was written specifically for publication.

It is possible to start with a private diary, journal or letter and use it like a first draft, adapting and modifying it for a more public version. Try it: write an entry in your private diary or journal; write about the same incident in a letter to a close friend; and finally write about the incident in a way that you would be happy to share with the rest of the class.

2 Keeping a reading journal or log is another way of using diaries and journals to help you reflect on books read privately and in class. You can use it to record your responses and to keep notes and rough jottings about characters and events, personal connections and reviews etc.

3 Diaries are also a very useful way of helping you to be organised, hence the popularity of personal organisers which are just big diaries! There are lots of dates that you will need to remember. Look through any diary and note what events are specially marked, e.g. full moons and Bank Holidays. Make a list of all the dates that you personally need to remember, e.g. holidays, birthdays, anniversaries, appointments. Design you own personal diary or year book and fill in these dates. It could be a large format to go on a wall or desk; it could be small enough to carry around with you. You might want

to illustrate it with pictures, photographs, drawings or sketches. Another way of illustrating it is with quotations or sayings. You could take a theme and design your diary around that, e.g. The Pooh Diary, The Conservation Diary, The Women's Diary. Have a look at some commercially produced diaries to get some ideas.

The class could design and fill in a large wall diary with all the relevant dates, e.g. visits, field trips, practicals, orals, exams, holidays.

4 Writing diaries, journals and letters based on characters in books or on real people is a way of relating to them and understanding them. Writing 'as if' you were them is a way of putting yourself in their shoes, and this may enable you to understand their actions and their motivation.

5 Another way of understanding a poem or a story is to write a diary or journal extract as if you were seeing it through the eyes of a minor character or an imagined character. Retelling the story from another point of view can often help clarify some of the issues.

Write a diary extract for Pete's sister, Susie describing how you felt when you discovered that someone had been reading your private diary.

6 Writing letters from characters, real or fictional, in books or poems to imagined people outside the book or poem, or between characters in the book or poem is another interesting and useful way of understanding what you have read.
- Write a letter from Maxine Harrison to Pete Payne offering him advice on his relationship with Cilla.
- Write a letter from Beryl Bainbridge to Susan Hill about living in the country and village life in Britain.